The Normativity of Musical Works

Art and Law

Volumes published in this Brill Research Perspectives title are listed at *brill.com/rpal*

The Normativity of Musical Works

A Philosophical Inquiry

By

Alessandro Arbo

BRILL

LEIDEN | BOSTON

This paperback book edition is simultaneously published as issue 4.2–3 (2020) of *Art and Law*, DOI:10.1163/24684309-12340011

Library of Congress Control Number: 2021903333

Typeface for the Latin, Greek, and Cyrillic scripts: "Brill". See and download: brill.com/brill-typeface.

ISBN 978-90-04-46276-2 (paperback)
ISBN 978-90-04-46277-9 (e-book)

This book is printed on acid-free paper and produced in a sustainable manner.

Contents

The Normativity of Musical Works

A Philosophical Inquiry

Alessandro Arbo
Université de Strasbourg, France
arbo@unistra.fr

Abstract

The cases of copyright infringement that occasionally crop up in the world of music raise many interesting questions: what do we mean when we talk about the identity of a musical work and what does such an identity involve? What in fact are the properties that make it something worth protecting and preserving? These issues are not only of legal relevance, they are central to a philosophical discipline that has seen considerable advances over the last few decades: musical ontology. Taking into account its main theoretical models, this essay argues that an understanding of the ontological status of musical works should acknowledge the irreducible ambivalence of music as an "art of the trace" and as a "performative art." It advocates a theory of the musical work as a "social object" and, more specifically, as a sound artefact that functions aesthetically and which is based on a trace informed by a normative value. Such a normativity is further explored in relation to three primary ways of conceiving and fixing the trace: orality, notation and phonography.

Keywords

musical work – musical performance – normativity – ontology – orality – phonography – copyrights

Introduction

What is a musical work? The answer seems almost too easy: it is a piece of music that is normally notated on a score and intended to be performed, sung, sometimes recorded, and ultimately listened to. But the moment we try to take a closer look at this answer, or to compare it with actual examples, questions

 | DOI:10.1163/9789004462779_002

begin to arise. Is a score necessary, for instance? Should we consider a traditional song, a popular nursery rhyme or a recorded song as being in the same category as a Beethoven symphony? If so, how can we distinguish such objects from the performances that are supposed to bring them to life? What are they really made of?

Philosophers have often asked such questions over the past few decades, sparking a debate that has seen a lively face-off between theoretical approaches and paradigms.[1] These debates have not always enthused musicologists, or even some philosophers, who have found them too abstract, too removed from experience[2] or history.[3] Yet, perhaps precisely because of their eminently speculative nature, they have had one considerable merit: that of subjecting the categories and concepts that structure our ways of looking at music to careful, finely argued analysis. By studying some of these debates, this essay proposes an examination of the nature of musical works and especially of their functioning in the present day. Emphasis will be laid on analysing the normativity on which their existence is based. I will begin by marking out the boundaries of this issue and highlighting its implications.

Like all artforms, music is imbued with rules or what are sometimes called "laws," which are usually based on rational or conventional principles. Ancient peoples were very much aware of this, as is evidenced by the interest shown by Ancient Greeks, Arabs, Indians and the Chinese in the mathematical relations underlying the principles of musical harmony. The Greeks gave the word *nome* (law) to short melodic themes they believed to be connected to a certain *ethos*, and where, according to Pseudo-Plutarch "it was unlawful to alter the pitch appointed for each one."[4] Indeed, each musical culture, ancient

1 Excellent summaries on the debate about the ontology of musical works can be found in essays by Sandrine Darsel, "Qu'est-ce qu'une œuvre musicale?," *Klesis. Revue philosophique* 13 (2009): 147–185; Carl Matheson and Ben Caplan, "Ontology," *The Routledge Companion of Philosophy and Music*, ed. Theodore Gracyk and Andrew Kania (London and New York: Routledge, 2011), 38–47; Andrew Kania, "The Philosophy of Music," *The Stanford Encyclopedia of Philosophy* (Fall 2012 Edition), ed. Edward N. Zalta. URL: http://plato.stanford.edu/archives/fall2012/entries/music/, §2; Lisa Giombini, *Musical Ontology. A Guide for the Perplexed* (Milano: Mimesis, 2017); Stephen Davies, "Works of Music: Approaches to the Ontology of Music from Analytic Philosophy," *Music Research Annual* 1, 2020: 1–19. URL: https://musicresearchannual.org/wp-content/uploads/2020/11/daviese28094works-of-music.pdf.

2 See Aaron Ridley, "Against Musical Ontology," *The Journal of Philosophy*, 4/2003, 203–230.

3 Lydia Goehr, *The Imaginary Museum of Musical Works. An Essay in the Philosophy of Music* (Oxford: Oxford University Press, 1992), 69–86. For further criticism, see Christopher Bartel, "Music without Metaphysics," *British Journal of Aesthetics* 51 (2011), 383–98; James O. Young, "The Poverty of Music Ontology," *Journal of Music and Meaning* 13 (2014/15), 1–19.

4 Pseudo-Plutarch, *Plutarch's Morals*, trans. by several hands, corrected and revised by William W. Goodwin, Boston. Little, Brown, and Company/Cambridge, Press of John Wilson & Son, 1874, 107.

or modern, has developed normative systems that define the scope of what is advisable, accepted, tolerated or proscribed within a given musical framework. However, I will only address this issue of normativity, which characterizes the definition of music languages, styles, or more fundamentally what has been termed "musical grammar,"[5] in a very limited manner. Likewise, I will also leave aside the question of the norms pertaining to the purchase or sale of recordings or scores as well as the opportunity (well documented since Plato) of regulating the ethical, political or religious function of certain types of music. Conversely, the focus will be on the normativity inherent in the very conception of musical works, and even in their creation and identification. The existence of a musical work, as we will see, implies the fixation of a trace and of a norm that will allow it to be reproduced and actualized in historical time. This fixation and this normativity will be my main focus here.

Why dwell on this? In music, and in art in general, the idea of a work whose connotations remain stable over time is very much outdated: the avant-gardes have brushed it aside by paving the way towards a more open, changing musical experience, beyond the limitations of its ritual presentation in concert form. In turn, postmodern poetics have contributed to challenging its identity, using quotation and collage as the basis of a diffuse creativity. Ultimately, everything seems to be working towards a dismantlement of the meaning of the musical work as an aesthetic unit – including, most recently, the rise of digital technologies and of the Internet – and foregrounding the breakdown of genre barriers[6] and the experience of the listener/viewer as creator.[7] Why, then, should we examine such an antiquated notion?

The answer is simple: it is because, upon closer examination, and despite appearances, we cannot truly do without it. Indeed, even if – or sometimes precisely because – the identity and existence of musical works are now problematic,[8] this can in no way be considered as a false problem. Evidence of this can be found in countless copyright cases, as well as, more broadly, each time where, in the context of an aesthetic evaluation or explanation, an identification of the properties of the musical object in question turns out to be indispensable.

5 See Mario Baroni, Rossana Dalmonte and Carlo Jacoboni, *Le regole della musica. Indagine sui meccanismi della comunicazione* (Torino: EDT, 1999), 13.

6 In the brochure for the 2016–2017 season of the Paris Philarmonie, Laurent Bayle wrote: "Our goal is to start breaking down barriers, which musical life desperately needs."

7 This trend is clearly on display in a number of recent installations and musical works, such as "Lullaby Experience" (2019) by French composer Pascal Dusapin.

8 See Stephen Davies, *Themes in the Philosophy of Music* (Oxford: Oxford University Press, 2003), 45–46.

A famous example illustrates this very concretely. In January 1973, the band Pink Floyd, who by then were already fixtures of the international progressive rock scene, recorded their eighth album *The Dark Side of the Moon* at Abbey Road Studios, London. On Sunday 21 January, they brought Clare Torry, an unknown British singer, into the studio to improvise a solo on one of the album's songs, "The Great Gig in the Sky." The session was a success: once her work was done, Torry left with the previously agreed fee of £30. A few months later, her performance was released in the fifth song of the published album. Thirty years later, in 2004, the singer sued Pink Floyd (and EMI) over unpaid royalties. The suit alleged that her part had contributed to the album's considerable success (it remains one of the biggest commercial hits of all time, with over 50 million copies sold). In 2005, she won an out-of-court settlement. Subsequent reissues of *The Dark Side of the Moon* credited her explicitly alongside keyboard player Richard Wright for her vocal contribution. It can be said that this case is mainly of legal and commercial interest. It is no less true, however, that it raises an ontological problem: on what grounds was what was initially an improvised performance should have been – and indeed was – recognised as a component of Pink Floyd's work? Can such recognition be given to *all* improvisations? When, and in what conditions, can a performance be considered as a *work*?

Numerous cases of copyright infringement documented in the legal literature raise similar issues. It must be acknowledged that the notion to which they refer, that of copyright, is not only relatively recent, but quite particular. Such a notion is based on the idea of property which, while being linked to an object that can be sold, remains inalienable; this shows to what extent a work of art is perceived "to be something different from ordinary objects, something which is different not just from an ontological point of view, but very often in terms of its value."[9] But above all, beyond its historical contingency, the phenomenon of copyright infringement highlights the problem of the identity of the objects concerned. When trying to establish whether or not George Harrison's "My Sweet Lord" copies Ronald Mack's "He's So Fine," one can certainly consider – as the judge did in the conclusions of this famous case – that Harrison had plagiarized in an unconscious or unintentional way.[10] What remains relevant here, beyond the evident similarity between the two songs, is to ask what was really at the centre of the dispute: what exactly is Mack's work that Harrison is

9 See Tiziana Andina, *What is Art? The Question of Definition Reloaded* (Leiden: Brill, 2017), 5–6.

10 See the *West's Federal Supplement print publication*, "Bright Tunes Music Corp. v. Harrisongs Music, Ltd" 420 F. Supp (1976) 181 (see, on the "Music Copyright Infringement Resource": https://cpb-us-w2.wpmucdn.com/blogs.law.gwu.edu/dist/a/4/files/2016/05/Brite-Tunes.pdf).

supposed to have plagiarized? Is it a (simple) melodic-harmonic structure or should we consider it to be the song as played or fixed on the record? Would we still be talking about plagiarism if instead of singing Harrison had made it an instrumental piece? What if he had changed its arrangement?

Those who produce, play, compose or judge music constantly face such conundrums. These situations reflect the extent to which we sometimes need to establish the status of the musical entities we are dealing with. I intend to go down this rabbit hole: my concern is to find out more about what should (and should not) be understood when we speak of musical work. I will attempt to unpack what a musical work is, the various situations where one might encounter one, establish what practices, relations and constraints it can (or must) draw on, and understand what kind of normativity its own existence as an artwork is based on. These questions should not be understood in an axiological sense, but in a philosophical sense (or, in some respects – to use a more controversial term – in a metaphysical sense). In other words, the point will not be to pass value judgments, even though the question of the value of the works, or more precisely of their critical assessment, will be taken into consideration – but to examine the criteria and rationales used to refer to them as such and to explain their aesthetic workings.

In particular I intend to demonstrate the following:

1) the concept of "work," rightly used to refer to a certain way of producing music in Europe since the early nineteenth century, relates to a more general principle, shared by most present and past musical cultures, consisting in attributing a normative value to a given sound structure;
2) an adequate understanding of this normativity requires awareness of music's irreducible ambivalence, split between the art of the trace[11] and the art of performance;
3) the normativity of musical works should be considered in strict relation to three main forms of expression of the musical trace: orality, notation and recording.

It is useful to focus on the most common meanings of the concepts and objects discussed here. In this regard, I should emphasise that the following generalisations should not be misconstrued as defending a principle of universality: rather, at this stage, I seek to heed Aristotle's call to examine what appears to apply "in all or most cases."[12] Whenever possible, case analyses will be complemented by clarification on the categories and criteria used for differentiating

11 On this notion see below, part 1, note 80, 25.

12 Aristotle, *Analitics II*, 30, 87b, 19–22; *Poetics*, 1451a 38–b12.

the phenomena examined. Whenever possible, moreover, I will follow a methodology that is now routinely termed "descriptivist"[13] in art ontology, building on Peter Frederick Strawson's distinction between "descriptive and revisionary metaphysics."[14] In short, this means considering the ways in which the objects and events examined are described by starting from common sense intuitions.[15] This will have to be done while keeping in mind the difficulties with which such a descriptive perspective is measured, and the fact that such intuitions may be in conflict with one another.[16] Conceptual suggestions or rectifications will be ruled out, but they shall be proposed mostly in cases where major issues, such as contradictions of principle, arise.

The first part of this essay will begin by exploring the role played by the concept of the work in musical discourse, and then reflect on the nature of what can be referred to by this term. This might appear to be an odd approach: how can we hope to consolidate knowledge about something that we are not entirely certain exists? This is admittedly a serious objection, but it is not insurmountable. If we reverse the terms of the equation, we might even note that before considering whether something exists, or how it exists, we need to come to an agreement about the thing whose existence we purport to ascertain or document. In any case, there is no reason to see both approaches as antithetical or exclusive: clarifying the categories on which we rely to describe, explain or even simply identify the phenomena or facts we are interested in is an indispensable prerequisite to viable knowledge-building. I will thus begin by taking this step, so as to offer a choice between multiple possible meanings of the concepts examined, and to consider their mutual relations. The choice in question will be based on reasoned arguments whilst clarifying the criteria that lead us to favour a given option over another. My hope is that this attempt will shed some light on the conceptual frameworks that underpin knowledge in the field of musicology. Once I have clarified these concepts, I will delve deeper into the nature and the properties of what I am hoping to define through them, namely musical works, and focus on how they actually work in the third part. The latter

13 See Andrew Kania, "The Methodology of Musical Ontology: Descriptivism and its Implications," *British Journal of Aesthetics* 48, n. 4 (2008): 426–444; Stephen Davies, "Works of Music: Approaches to the Ontology of Music from Analytic Philosophy," 5–6.

14 Peter Frederick Strawson, *Individuals: An Essay in Descriptive Metaphysics* (London and New York: Routledge, 1959), 9.

15 Roger Pouivet, *Philosophie du rock. Une ontologie des artefacts et des enregistrements* (Paris: Presses Universitaires de France, 2010), 73.

16 See Marcello Ruta, "Is there an Ontological Musical Common Sense?," *Aisthesis* (Special issue: *Ontologie musicali*, ed. Alessandro Arbo and Alessandro Bertinetto) 6 (2013), 67–86; Giombini, *Musical Ontology*, 317.

examines in greater detail the three aforementioned forms of fixation of the trace and of the normativity of musical works: orality, notation, and recording.

1 Works and Performances

1.1 *Sounds and Music*

Talking about musical works means talking about a certain way of making music. Before we even get to the heart of our subject, it may be useful to take a more general view and specify what kind of phenomena we mean by the term "music." In fact, although these two issues are different and can be dealt with independently,[17] they still show a certain permeability. It goes without saying that such an issue is broad and certainly cannot be resolved in the few lines that follow;[18] they may serve as a simple, necessary and quick introductory framework for the issue that we are most interested in dealing with here: that of knowing what we mean when we speak of a musical work.

Music, it has often been said, is the art of sounds. If we take this definition as our starting point, we might be tempted to consider music primarily from a purely physical standpoint, i.e. sounds. This is understandable since without sounds there would probably be no music. However, knowing what a sound is (or its physical causes such as the length of a string, the intensity of its vibration, as well as the spectral composition of the resulting sound to its waveform and the speed of its propagation in the air) would never bring us face to face with the kind of entities we call "musical." To put it bluntly, musical entities do not coincide with physical objects or events. So how can we account for them?

First of all, for there to be music, there must be a human who hears – or even a human who *listens* (who intentionally orients or directs their attention and their ears towards something). A sound can only be considered "musical" when it is perceived. It could then be viewed as an object captured within a framework that constitutes a reality in itself, distinct from any physical reality: this is what philosophers call an "intentional object."[19] From this perspective,

17 Jerrold Levinson, *Music, Art and Metaphysics. Essays in Philosophical Aesthetics* (Oxford: Oxford University Press, 2011) 269.

18 The topic has been dealt with in more detail and from different perspectives by Levinson, *Music, Art and Metaphysics*, 267–278; Andy Hamilton, *Aesthetics and Music* (London, Continuum, 2007) 40–65; Jean-Jacques Nattiez, "Pluralité et diversité du savoir musical," in *Musiques. Une encyclopédie pour le XXI*e *siècle. 2 Les savoirs musicaux*, ed. Jean-Jacques Nattiez (Arles/Paris: Actes Sud/Cité de la musique, 2004), 17–24.

19 Roger Scruton, *The Aesthetics of Music* (Oxford: Clarendon Press, 1997), 78–79.

its way of being resembles that of a "pure" event, similar to the one Pierre Schaeffer was aiming at with his idea of "acousmatic listening."[20]

In this context, the adjective "intentional" does not have the same meaning as in a legal sense, where it indicates a type of voluntary action; nor does it limit itself to designating what is "about something" but, more particularly (starting with Franz Brentano and the phenomenologists, who adopted an interpretation of medieval scholasticism), a key characteristic of consciousness. This term distinguishes psychic facts from transcendental ideals and physical facts. To say that a psychic fact or ideality is 'intentional' means that it contains something as an object, albeit in different ways (such as a belief, judgment, perception, consciousness, desire, hatred, etc.). Thus, a diminished seventh chord is not the (simple) result of the wave-like movements that vibrating bodies impart to a portion of air; rather, it consists of a certain representation of a set of sounds that we hear in the form of a diminished seventh chord, with well-determined and recognizable relational properties and characteristics (it is a chromatic alteration of the dominant chord, an enharmonic chord, etc.).

This approach has its advantages, but it is not free of difficulties. It has the merit of highlighting the (relative) autonomy of the object we are interested in: when a melody seems to "move" in a certain way – when it seems to us to be moving towards a goal, or to be slowing down, etc. – in order to understand its movement we don't need to think about the physical causes that gave rise to it. It should be made clear once again that such causes do exist, but that they do not (at least directly) account for the musical phenomenon *per se*. Thus, when I hear the ascending movement of a melody, it is of no help to me to know that the physical movement required for its production is indeed ascending (this is often not the case, and it is even quite the opposite: to produce a higher note on a cello the hand must descend the fingerboard; to "ascend" on a keyboard one must move horizontally to the right, etc.). Musical perception implies the reference to an imaginative world based on causality of a different order.[21] Strictly speaking, this explanation avoids physicalist reductionism: what we consider as having the attributes of a musical entity – for example, the suspension of an interrupted cadence (V–VI) – can be explained by its own logic.

Once we accept that musical objects are intentional objects based on transcendental principles, then any phenomenological approach (or one involving the philosophy of mind) will be concerned with theorizing first their ideality

20 Pierre Schaeffer, *Traité des objets musicaux. Essai interdisciplines* (Paris: Editions du Seuil, 1977; 1st edition: 1966).

21 Francis Wolff admirably expanded upon this topic in *Pourquoi la musique?* (Paris: Fayard, 2015), 67–77.

(as aesthetic objects), and second, their anchoring in the anthropological foundation of a *Lebenswelt*. In the end, everything rests on the assumption that we can refer to a world of representations (but also of desires, expectations, etc.) which, without necessarily depending on external causes, is common to us. Based on this perspective, how can we explain the fact that we are able to recognize music within the infinite universe of sounds? A sound is perceived as musical when we recognize certain structures in it: basically, we hear it as having a certain pitch and a certain duration in relation to other sounds. This leads to the idea of the existence, in our perception, of a kind of pre-musical "sound space" where the principles of organization used by all musical cultures are rooted.[22] But how can the transition to higher levels be explained? Why what is recognised as melodic, or melodically correct, in a Turkish *taqsim* is not recognised as being melodic in a Palestrina motet or in an Indian *raga*?

It has been argued that, despite the many ways in which sounds can be organized, there is a specific and common mode of organization to which we have given the name "music." For example, it is possible to argue, as the German musicologist Hugo Riemann did, for the existence of "musical logic."[23] However, this viewpoint runs the risk of prioritizing (more or less explicitly) the logic of the so-called Western musical language. More fundamentally, an attempt has been made to show that, in order to be able to speak of music, it is necessary for the sound to be understood as a "tone," i.e. within a grid or a "sound space" that is segmented into discrete units[24] (a fact that would be clearly perceptible in a Gregorian mode as well as in an Indian *raga*). It would thus be possible to highlight the presence in various musical civilizations of similar strategies in organizing sounds, that is to say, the use of discrete pitches and rhythmic organization. We may nevertheless wonder whether such features would be sufficient to explain what makes a sound sequence properly musical. In many cultures, an important indication of musicality often consists of melodic or vocal inflections that fall outside a precise grid of pitches. In other words, one might say that what is musical is found between the notes, not in the notes. Moreover, several types of music based on the transformation of timbre (as in *concrète*, electronic, acousmatic and aleatory music) would then be considered as being exceptions. For some, that is indeed the conclusion we should draw, possibly adopting, for these phenomena, the alternative label of "sonic arts." Insofar as a significant part of the evolution of 20th century Western music can

22 Giovanni Piana, *Filosofia della musica* (Milano, Guerini, 1990), 188–213.

23 Hugo Riemann, *Musikalishe Logik. Hauptzüge der physiologischen und psychologischen Begründung unseres Musiksystems* (Leipzig: Kahnt, 1874).

24 This idea has been robustly argued by Scruton, *The Aesthetics of Music*, 19–79.

be explained in terms of a shift from the paradigm of the note to the paradigm of sound,[25] this solution may still leave us somewhat unsatisfied.

In short, it could be better to admit that "music" is a sort of conceptual fog whose limits would be futile to establish once and for all. Or that what we call music, as Luciano Berio suggested, is perhaps nothing more than the search for a constantly repressed frontier.[26] Knowing when and how such a repression occurs is another matter, and is certainly much more complex. It is no less true that what we call "music" manifests a certain selection or delineation made by a group of people within the wider horizon of audible sounds. In other words, following Jean-Jacques Nattiez' efficient formula, it is the "sound produced and organised by a culture."[27] What we can say about musical works should not contradict this general principle; on the contrary, it should succeed in specifying one of the ways in which the musical work manifests itself.

1.2 *On the Concept of Musical Work*

While the term "opus" began to be used to refer to musical compositions in the Renaissance era (its first occurrence is found in the writings of German theoretician Nikolaus Listenius[28]), scholars have generally focused on the meaning it acquired during the Classical-Romantic period, when a range of beliefs and institutional frameworks reinforced the centrality (and prestige) of the composer's work. The *Werkbegriff* ("work-concept") then came to prevail as an aesthetic paradigm of Western music:[29] as Lydia Goehr put it, it became the main "regulative concept" of musical practice.[30] The socio-historical context of its dissemination was the creation of cultural and recreative institutions by a bourgeoisie that was asserting its dominance in the West.[31] Against that backdrop, music earned the status of an autonomous artform, freed from the more functional or ancillary role it had previously played. Its products became

25 See Makis Solomos, *De la musique au son. L'émergence du son dans la musique des XX*ᵉ*–XXI*ᵉ *siècles* (Rennes: Presses Universitaires de Rennes, 2013).

26 Luciano Berio, *Intervista sulla musica*, ed. Rossana Dalmonte (Roma-Bari: Laterza, 1981), 7.

27 Nattiez, "Pluralité et diversité du savoir musical," 24.

28 See Michela Garda, "Le teorie dell'opera d'arte musicale nel Novecento," in *Storia dei concetti musicali. Espressione, forma, opera*, ed. Gianmario Borio and Carlo Gentili (Roma: Carocci, 2007), 247–248.

29 Carl Dahlhaus, *Esthetics of Music*, trans. William W. Austin (Cambridge: Cambridge University Press, 1982), 11–15.

30 Goehr, *The Imaginary Museum of Musical Works*, 109.

31 The connection between the concept of art and the affirmation of the idea of aesthetic autonomy in bourgeois institutions was emphasized by Adorno's dialectic approach; see Theodor Wiesengrund Adorno, *Aesthetic Theory*, ed. Gretel Adorno and Rolf Tiedemann, trans. by Robert Hullot-Kentor (London – New York: Continuum, 2002), 225.

"cultural goods," liable to be appreciated in concert halls, in an experience reminiscent of museum visits.[32] They were considered as the product of a creative mind, bearing the signature of an artist – the composer – who took it upon himself (as Beethoven did) to sort and classify them within an authorized catalogue. They were to be considered as the result of free creative activity, and even, for the most exemplary, of genius. This vision gave rise to a value system that was meant to last, as over two centuries later it still characterizes global musical culture:[33] at the top, we have a "creative" act, and multiple acts of "performance" are expected to safeguard its authenticity by addressing a crowd of listeners at the bottom of the scale, who should reap its benefits in religious silence. To speak (properly) of musical works, we should then draw on the historical frameworks of Western music, from Beethoven to the contemporary era. The concept should be understood as the catalyst of the division of labour between a composer notating ideas on a score, the performers who implement these ideas faithfully (the so-called *Werktreue* ideal) and an audience seated in a concert hall to share an aesthetic experience of an object, the work, which has been assigned a high artistic value.[34]

This option has undeniable advantages, allowing as it does, especially, to avoid anachronisms or misuses of the concept. Neither Plato nor Confucius ever attended a concert with a paying audience: it would therefore be wrong to claim that they experienced these original, high-value objects that we call "musical works." On what grounds could we actually consider a Mongolian throat singing performance or a blues number by Big Bill Broonzy (recorded by Alan Lomax in the 1950s[35]) to be a "musical work" as such? Most ethnomusicologists have significant reservations on the subject. They have all but banished the term "musical work" from their vocabulary, as they see it as ill-suited to describing what they encounter in the field, be that songs, hymns, dances, prayers, etc.

While this "strict" approach to the concept prevents us from making the unfortunate mistake – which some might term "neo-colonialist," "ethnocentric," "Eurocentric" or even "racist" – of applying our own conceptions of music

32 The type of experience implied by the form of organization of contemporary musical culture was explained by Hans Georg Gadamer; see Alessandro Arbo, *Il suono instabile. Saggi sulla filosofia della musica nel Novecento* (Torino: Trauben, 2000), 103–123.

33 See Nicholas Cook, *Music: A Very Short Introduction* (Oxford: Oxford University Press, 2000), 13–14.

34 See Walter Wiora, *Das musikalische Kunstwerk* (Tutzing: Hans Schneider, 1983) and Wilhelm Seidel, *Werk und Werkbegriff in der Musikgeschichte* (Darmstadt: Wissenschaftliche Buchgesellschaft, 1987).

35 See the recordings published on the website of The Association for Cultural Equity (ACE): http://research.culturalequity.org/get-audio-ix.do?ix=session&id=BB52&idType=abbrev&sortBy=abc.

to distant traditions, its unconditional embrace is also somewhat perplexing in some respects. One might start by distinguishing value judgments from factual descriptions. Indeed, some musical productions that fall outside of the aforementioned scope may seemingly not be designed to be judged as artistic outputs of a creative mind. Yet, would it be accurate to claim that this condition should be met for the word "work" to apply? While the etymology of the word clearly refers to the idea of labour, both in English and German, very often, in art, "calling something a work amounts to refusing to treat it as an ordinary product (except in the French technical terminology of architecture, with its distinction between *gros oeuvre* and *second oeuvre*)."[36] The term "artwork" thus seems to imply a distinction between what is recognised to have value and what generally isn't recognised as such. This applies to music: calling a composition a "work" is putting it on a pedestal. In other words, we use it to refer to something that has a value of its own – or that is considered as likely to have high value in the eyes of a number of individuals. Should we deduce from this that every musical work is an exceptional achievement? This is in a sense Theodor Adorno's argument in his *Aesthetic Theory*:

> The concept of an artwork implies that of its success. Failed artworks are not art: Relative success is alien to art; the average is already the bad. The average is incompatible with the medium of particularization. Middling artworks, the healthy soil of minor masters so appreciated by historians of a similar stamp, presuppose an ideal similar to what Lukács had the audacity to defend as a "normal artwork." However, being the negation of the spurious universal of the norm, art tolerates neither normal works nor middling ones that correspond to a norm or establish their meaning in terms of their distance to it.[37]

Thus we are called to draw a line between high art, the true art that can aspire to the status of truth, and what simply is not that (or what masquerades as that). Adorno, as we know, was quite adept at this. But is it necessary for a musical work to be high art?

Actually, although there is a form of evaluation and appreciation at work in the way in which we perceive musical works (and artworks, of course), and even supposing that what is recognised as artistic does not suffer what is normal or middling (a condition that may require us to reject a number of pieces

---

36 Jacques Morizot, "Œuvre," in *Dictionnaire d'esthétique et de philosophie de l'art*, ed. Jacques Morizot and Roger Pouivet (Paris: Armand Colin, 2012²), 337–338.

37 Adorno, *Aesthetic Theory*, 188.

by Vivaldi or Rossini, and even perhaps by the divine Mozart), this way of looking at things is not entirely reliable. One simply needs to go to a concert, to visit a gallery or attend an opening to witness the extent to which the class of artworks is populated by products that cannot aspire to the status of a masterpiece. It also remains to be seen whether ordinary products can be considered as works. Think of the infinity of statuettes, vases, medallions, bronzes, glass ornaments, stone sculptures, etc. found in most museums worldwide, or, to stick to our area of interest here, the melodies and rhythms associated with everyday situations, military marches, hymns, songs used in sport events, weddings, political rallies, schools, places of worship that we find in most cultures. These productions may often be modest or unoriginal, but is this enough to deny them the status of works?

It is not easy to answer yes. The value of the aforementioned ordinary products is often more of a ritual, religious or political nature than aesthetic. Yet, not to mention that the same goes for many masterpieces by great composers, there is no real reason why these products should be denied artistic value simply because the experience they are designed to elicit is insufficiently autonomous. Indeed, the notion of the autonomy of art often goes hand in hand with the notion that art can create an experience founded on a pleasure which, in his analytic of the beautiful, Kant had defined (admittedly without exclusively or mainly referring to art) as "disinterested."[38] However – leaving aside the fact that if we take this reasoning to its logical conclusion, there is no longer any real reason to claim that some objects are intrinsically unaesthetic[39] –, the idea that an aesthetic attitude should be associated with a particular type of disinterested perception does not seem tenable. There are likelier explanations, such as different levels of motivation in our attention to objects,[40] or, more precisely, a change in the functioning of cognitive activities that ultimately appears to make the concept of "aesthetic conduct" more relevant.[41]

Perhaps a simpler approach is to consider, when we seek to establish whether an object is part of the class of artistic objects, if in ordinary contexts, that object is characterized by an aesthetic form of symbolic functioning.

---

38 Immanuel Kant, *Critique of Judgement*, trans. by James Creed Meredith, ed. Nicholas Walker (Oxford and New York: Oxford University Press, 2007), 37.

39 Jerome Stolnitz, *Aesthetics and Philosophy of Art Criticism* (Boston: Houghton Mifflin, 1960), 32–42.

40 This is the main critical remark formulated by George Dickie, "The Myth of the Aesthetic Attitude," *American Philosophical Quarterly*, Vol. 1, No. 1 (Jan. 1964), 56–65.

41 Jean-Marie Schaeffer, *Les célibataires de l'Art. Pour une esthétique sans mythes* (Paris: Gallimard, 1996), 152–153.

As explained by Nelson Goodman,[42] symptoms revealing such a functioning include the syntactic and semantic density of the signs that characterize it, as well as their capacity to exemplify and manifest multiple and complex references. There is no need to summon a Mahler symphony to illustrate this: a folk song is enough to make the presence of at least some of these symptoms manifest. Take a famous song like "Bella Ciao"; is not its melodic curve (emphasizing a minor sixth and the insistent repetition of the word "ciao") a perfect symbol liable to exemplify and manifest multiple and complex references? Reportedly, it was only after the war that this song, whose origins were inaccurately traced back to the *mondine* of Padania, became the symbol of the *resistenza* and the struggle against Fascism and Nazism. It should also be noted that the very same song was the symbol of other very diverse causes and events: from protests against the crackdown on freedom of expression[43] to a political victory of the French left,[44] a heist symbolizing the struggle against the economic power of banks,[45] a memorial for the victims of a terrorist attack,[46] and who knows how many other settings.

This in no way means that all musical objects are equal in value: certainly, there are works that manifest a higher value than others, or whose symbolic functioning manifests a higher degree of complexity, calling more attention to the symbols themselves than to what they refer. Yet, just recalling that in his symphonies, Mahler extensively drew on military marches, folk melodies or nursery rhymes – without necessarily seeking to make them nobler, as Adorno's musical physiognomy taught us[47] – is enough to make us suspect that there is no basic difference between a symphony and a folk tune. In other words, there is no reason to deny these melodies the status of works, or to consider as exceedingly bold the idea that there might be something akin to a "normal" art.

How can we detect such a functioning when we experience music? In most civilizations, listening to music – or, more broadly, responding to its prompts, with a gesture, a movement of the body, a dance step or other behaviours – means not only appreciating the act of someone who is expected to play or

42 Nelson Goodman, *Ways of Worldmaking* (Hassocks: The Harvester Press, 1978), 67–68.

43 In 2002, it was sung by journalist Michele Santoro at the beginning of the TV show "Sciuscià" in response to Silvio Berlusconi's "*editto bulgaro*."

44 The song was sung at the end of François Hollande's speech after winning the 2012 French presidential election.

45 In the second season finale of the Spanish TV show "La Casa de Papel" ("Money Heist"), created by Álex Pina and broadcast on Antena 3 and Netflix.

46 The actor and comedian Christophe Alévêque sang the song at a memorial for the victims of the Charlie Hebdo killings (France 2 evening news, 11 January 2015).

47 Theodor Wiesengrund Adorno, *Mahler. A Musical Physiognomy*, trans. Edmund Jephcott (Chicago and London, University of Chicago Press, 1996).

sing, but also, grasping, thanks to such an act or through such an act, preexisting musical units that the musician is expected to perform. Indeed, while Plato did not experience works in the modern sense of the term, it is quite likely that when he went to the theatre or listened to a rhapsodist, he knew how to distinguish a paean from a hymen or a threnody; it is also equally likely that he knew how to distinguish a particular paean from other paeans he knew or had heard. How are we to do justice to this form of appreciation without forcing musical reality into the Procrustean bed of a category that owes this much to Western modern history?

One strategy consists in relaxing the conditions to qualify for this category. As previously noted, a "minimal" condition for something to present itself as a musical work is that it should function aesthetically. Say that all music functions in this way; we need an additional criterion to delineate the category. Here is one: an object that functions aesthetically simply consists in a re-instantiable musical structure, meaning, roughly speaking, a structure that is likely to be identified across multiple presentations. This is the solution proposed in the pluralist and descriptivist model of Stephen Davies[48] which I will adopt here. While I do not deny the specific connotations acquired by *Workbegriff* in the historical settings where it emerged and developed, I will use it in a more flexible sense, to refer to any piece of music that is susceptible to being re-identified. In that sense, there is no need for a score, a concert hall or audience members sitting in numbered seats in order to speak of a musical work: the term may apply equally to a motet by Palestrina, a nursery rhyme (like "Twinkle, Twinkle, Little Star"), a cello suite by Bach or a Friulian *villotta* ("Al cjante il gjal"), a Led Zeppelin album (*Physical Graffiti*, 1975) or a Daft Punk hit ("Get Lucky," 2013). Of course, while these entities manifest an aesthetic functioning, they do so in rather different ways, including through an actual performance, for instance, or more frequently these days, a recording. I will elaborate on these differences later.[49] Having evidenced them, I will be led to stray from Davies's ontological model up to a point. Before that, I will define the boundaries of the category in more detail and examine the nature of the objects/events it allows us to designate.

1.3 *Improvised Music*

Performing or reproducing a song, a dance or a sonata are very common ways to make music, but they should not be considered as the only way to make

48 Stephen Davies, *Musical Works and Performances: a Philosophical Exploration* (Oxford: Oxford University Press, 2001), 19; Stephen Davies, "Works of Music: Approaches to the Ontology of Music from Analytic Philosophy," 2.

49 See below, part 3.

music. A musician practicing an instrument, or an individual whistling in the shower are not necessarily performing works: their activity might be exempt from such a requirement. Admittedly, it is rather easy to rule out cases such as these, where music practice does not appear to coincide with an explicit intention to play for someone and to get a result that may have some artistic value for them. It might however be more difficult to rule out others, especially when the musicians' activity is directed at a listener and reflects such an intention, but without the recognizable presence of an existing piece. This is the case of so-called "improvised" music, a label that encompasses a wide range of practices found in cultures that preceded the rise of technical reproducibility, in jazz (whose roots and development are intertwined with those of phonography),[50] and in many other practices using means of electronic and digital amplification and treatment of sound (the broad field of what is sometimes called "experimental music," often based on the combined use of acoustic and electronic instruments, with real-time sound processing), as well as some futurist experiments, the 1960s' happenings and a variety of music installations whose ephemeral quality is sometimes reminiscent of the experiments of environmental art. In these experiences, the idea of encountering a predefined musical object takes the back seat or is replaced by the intention of inducing a certain attitude in an individual who might be defined as an "artist-listener" or "artist-viewer." Should we include all these experiences in the class of musical works or exclude them?

Let us try to frame the question more clearly in order to answer it. I think we can easily agree on one point: if in delineating the category of work we emphasize the question of artistic value or aesthetic functioning, there is reason to consider that an improvised performance – say, a solo by John Coltrane, Keith Jarrett or Chick Corea, or a Pan Sonic concert – is a work. Yet, these are not the only questions at stake here and recognised as such. The idea of a musical work I have outlined involves the presence of a piece of music that preexists the act of performance: what in some musical practices is called a "composition," and is normally distinguished from "improvisation," which happens instantaneously and spontaneously. However, according to some scholars, this difference is not sufficient to justify a distinction in principle. This is argued, for instance, by Philip Alperson, the author of an early landmark paper in 1984 on the subject in the context of analytic aesthetics. Based on the premise that each composition implies a performance (even if only a mental one), Alperson suggests considering improvisation as "an activity of spontaneous

50 See Evan Eisenberg, *The Recording Angel: Music, Records and Culture from Aristotle to Zappa* (New Haven and London: Yale University Press, 2005), 117–120.

music-making in which the improviser somehow practices simultaneously the interdependent functions of composition and performance."[51] In turn, Peter Kivy called attention to the fact that both a composition and an improvisation involve the discovery of sound structures that should be considered as ideal entities, existing outside of space and time.[52] By analysing two tracks from Bill Evans' LP *Conversations with Myself* (1963), Steve Larson showed that certain improvisations should be considered as real compositions and, conversely, certain compositions as improvisations.[53] From a very different perspective, Sandrine Darsel[54] suggests that improvisations should be conceived as "works in action," in which the improviser should be considered as an "instant author." An improvisation would then be defined as the instantaneous creation or invention of a musical work.

It is true that there is a great deal of conceptual permeability between composition and improvisation. However, I believe that it is impossible to ignore some important differences between these two phenomena. The problem is that an improvisation, even if it draws on past elements or structures, is normally conceived, both by the improviser and the listener, as an action aimed at producing results that are not meant to correspond, at least beyond a certain point, to a pre-existing musical unit endowed with a normative value – or, most importantly, to have any prescriptive value. I use the qualifying phrase "beyond a certain point" because in many improvised musical practices, the musician is expected to be able to reproduce pre-existing elements. An example of this, often mentioned by Lee B. Brown,[55] is found in the Iranian *radif*, where the musician must master several hundred melodic units before he starts improvising on them. Additionally, in a number of cultures and musical genres, starting with jazz, the idea of improvisation implies the reinvention, and not simply the reproduction, of what has already been done. This means – if we look at this from the perspective of a listener who is accustomed to these

---

51 Philippe Alperson, "On Musical Improvisation," *Journal of Aesthetics and Art Criticism* 43, no. 1 (1984): 20. See also similar arguments in Daniele Goldoni, "Composizione e improvvisazione: dove sta la differenza?," *Aisthesis*, vol. 6, n. 3 (2013), 133–153. Alperson's thesis was criticized by Paul Vincent Spade, in "Do Composers Have To Be Performers Too?" *Journal of Aesthetics and Art Criticism* 49 (1991), 365–9, where he points out variations in the meanings given to the terms "composition" and "performance."

52 Peter Kivy, "Platonism in Music: A Kind of Defense," *Grazer Philosophische Studien* 19 (1983), 109–29.

53 Steve Larson, "Composition Versus Improvisation?," *Journal of Music Theory* 49, 2 (Fall 2005) 241–275.

54 Darsel, "Qu'est-ce qu'une œuvre musicale?," 176.

55 Lee B. Brown, "Improvisation," in *The Routledge Companion of Philosophy and Music*, ed. Theodore Gracyk and Andrew Kania (London and New York: Routledge, 2011), 60.

musical practices – that the salient aesthetic properties of an improvisation will differ from those of a composition: in the former, imperfections that would be more disruptive in the latter may be "forgiven" (a repetitive harmonic structure, a barely suggested melodic formula, a rhythm with little variation,[56] etc.) but something extra is expected (an ability to surprise us by taking risks, through instrumental gestures, formulas or digressions, etc.).[57] Even if in a sense one could say that "Classical era" variations in score form "suffer" from the same conditions, what is presented as improvisation has to correspond to a variation process in real time, without having the possibility of correcting errors, but instead having the need to know how to exploit them.

We have to recognise, then, that an improvising musician is engaged in an act that should be considered as mildly distinct from what happens in a composition. Above all, as has often been mentioned, there is a difference in temporality that is far from secondary. Unlike the composer, the improviser is not only unable to take time to revise or correct, but, as Lee B. Brown has observed, they must produce responses to something that has just been done on the spot; in that sense, the improviser's art is "a continuous feedback loop, such that later phrases are responses to previous ones."[58] Of course, what came before does condition composers too; but unlike improvisers, they generally have time to correct their work. As Clément Canonne aptly put it, the difference between an act of composition and an act of improvisation is that "where the composer *chooses what is needed*, i.e., he prescribes through his choice, the improviser, on the other hand, must choose: he *needs to choose*."[59]

As it happens, while composition and improvisation cannot be considered as equivalent, the category of work is mainly associated with the former. For what reasons, though? One might argue that this is basically a question of convention or terminological custom, but I do not believe this to be the case. As I have previously stated, the term "work" relates to the idea of a structure that

---

56 It might be argued that the repetitive left-hand rhythmic figures and the reiterations of the A minor/G major harmonic succession in Part I of Keith Jarrett's *Köln Concert* are failings that showcase the virtue (or genius) of the improvising pianist.

57 The difference – sometimes based on ethical arguments – between improvisations and works has been extensively addressed in Lee B. Brown, "Musical Works, Improvisation, and the Principle of Continuity," *Journal of Aesthetics and Art Criticism*, vol. 54, 1996, pp. 353–369; Alessandro Bertinetto, "Paganini Does Not Repeat. Improvisation And The Type/Token Ontology," *Teorema* XXXI/3 (2012) 105–126; Clément Canonne, "Sur l'ontologie de l'improvisation," in *Ontologie musicale*, ed. Alessandro Arbo and Marcello Ruta, 279–320.

58 Brown, "Improvisation," 65.

59 Canonne, "Sur l'ontologie de l'improvisation," 291. It could be added that this is true even when he "decides in advance *not to decide*"; see Jerrold Levinson, *Musical Concerns. Essays in Philosophy of Music* (Oxford: Oxford University Press, 2015) 149.

is expected to manifest a degree of longevity and a certain prescriptive value (both characteristics are strictly bound together). In the case of performing arts such as music or theatre, this longevity is ensured by creating a trace that will enable future repeat performances.[60] This is not the case, for instance, in performances of Indian, free jazz or hard trance music. Admittedly, in these three cases, one might argue that the sonic outcome of the musician's act is not entirely free. Indeed, such an outcome will be expected by a listener who has the skills to appreciate its allusions to pre-existing schemes or patterns: in the first of these three cases, the pre-existing schemes or patterns would be constituted by the *raga*; in the second these would be constituted by original formulas, or at least not overly naïve ones; and in the third, constituted by sounds or sound manipulations resulting from the use of a particular kind of sampler. Would we, however, be ready to allow that these schemes or patterns fit the definition of what we call "works"? In my view, taking such a stance would take us too far from the common meaning of the term, to the extent that it would make its use vague or meaningless. Perhaps we might more usefully note that, in the aforementioned improvisations, the work coincides with what the musician is able to produce using these preexisting elements, but I believe this would also be pushing the concept too far. Actually, this sort of output, even if it is accompanied by a great deal of constraints or norms and can appear as constructed as a composition,[61] is not intended to be prescriptive and, by its very nature, does not seek reproduction or longevity.

To demonstrate this, let us take a canonical example, one often used to test the soundness of theories of improvisation in jazz: Keith Jarrett's *Köln Concert*. This improvisation was recorded and released on a record that proved to be immensely successful.[62] The result bears the explicit signature of its author (one could not say the same of a recording of a traditional Indian music improvisation, where usually the performer lays no claim to authorship). The recording makes this performance re-instantiable: if we think of how this music is considered in the context of its reception,[63] we might say that it is indeed Jarrett's "work." However, looking more closely at these contexts, this

60 This applies to a lesser extent to a dance, where notation has undoubtedly played a smaller role than in music: see Frédéric Pouillaude, "D'une graphie qui ne dit rien. Les ambiguïtés de la notation chorégraphique," *Poétique* 137 n. 1 (2004), 99–123.

61 See Larson, "Composition Versus Improvisation?," 273.

62 The recording was released in 1975 by the ECM label. As of 2008, it had sold over 3.5 million copies (Corinna da Fonseca Wollheim, "A Jazz Night to Remember. The unique magic of Keith Jarrett's 'The Köln Concert'," *The Wall Street Journal* April 11, 2008).

63 In jazz, Eisenberg observes in *The Recording Angel*, 123 "the record is the work." This idea is shared by, among others, Vincenzo Caporaletti, *I processi improvvisativi nella musica. Un approccio globale* (Lucca: LIM, 2005), 80.

conclusion does not seem so irrefutable. In jazz, an improvisation does not in principle set out to leave a lasting trace: it is an instantaneous creation, situated in a given time and space (it is worth noting that jazz improvisations are often named after the place where they were created, as is the Jarrett case here). This is admittedly what happens in many ephemeral arts. But while a sand sculpture will last as long as it lasts, it exists at least for a certain amount of time. Many contemporary electronic music installations are made to last for the duration of a festival or exhibition, and then often become recorded documents. Our approach to such artefacts actually seems different to our approach to improvisation: even if we know the installation to be temporary, we attribute a specific constructive intention to its creator. This attribution is precisely what appears to change in the case of an improvisation: knowing it has been constructed or composed risks compromising our experience of it, which is more about going with the flow than piecing together the elements of a sonic structure.[64]

It is also true that, in the case of an improvisation that is based on a given outline, the intention of producing a complete expressive actualization of that outline could be considered as "functionally equivalent to the intention of making a work."[65] For this equivalent to be considered effective, we need to identify a means of transforming the improvisation into an artefact whose authorship is ensured and that can be reproduced. A Jarrett recording might appear to fully meet these conditions: by approving its release, the musician has allowed us to consider the recording as a finished result (a bootleg recording would lead us to a different conclusion). However, the final product of these transformations, although it is perfectly well re-identifiable strictly speaking, is not meant for performing. No matter, one might retort, as it is a phonographic work. Yet, if we look into the functions of this recording more closely, I believe it qualifies more as the document of a singular performance (whose meaning is at the same time that of a performative and creative act) rather than as the construction of a phonographic work.[66]

---

64 Clément Canonne, "L'appréciation esthétique de l'improvisation," *Aisthesis. Pratiche, Linguaggi e Saperi dell'estetico*, vol. 6 n. 3, 2013, 331–356.

65 Justin London, "Ephemeral Media, Ephemeral Works, and Sonny Boy Williamson's 'Little Village'," *The Journal of Aesthetics and Art Criticism*, vol. 71/1, 2013, 49.

66 I agree with Andrew Kania's remarks about the meaning of recorded improvisations in the jazz tradition; see Andrew Kania, "Works, Recordings, Performances: Classical, Rock, Jazz," in *Recorded Music. Philosophical and Critical Reflections*, ed. Mine Dogantan-Dack (London: Middlesex University Press, 2008), 12–15. The category of "phonographic work" and its scope will be discussed in greater detail in part 3.

Further, one might note that this improvisation, as other famous ones, was painstakingly transcribed, a transcription that has served as the basis for subsequent performances. In such cases, however, the gap between the descriptive value of the transcription and the prescriptive value of a score remains difficult to fill, unless the author has provided specific instructions.[67] The latter case involves another criterion for appreciation: in a successful performance of a transcribed improvisation, we look for aesthetic properties that differ from the original on which it is based (such as compliance with the instructions and the living and breathing character of a given dynamic or phrasing, for instance, not whimsical melodic or harmonic invention). This difference in perspective may to a certain extent explain some dissatisfied reactions to the "performances" of this transcription that can be found online.[68] In this sense, it seems more appropriate to speak of a performance of a *work based on an improvisation* by Jarrett (or in some cases of a cover,[69] when the pianist takes a few liberties) rather than of a performance of Jarrett's work.

In an attempt to gain a clearer idea of what mainly distinguishes an improvisation from a work, let us take a Beethoven sonata. When we listen to it, what we focus on is not a passing event, but an object that lasts over time. The Polish philosopher Roman Ingarden was probably the first to devote a comprehensive study (completed in the 1950s) to the nature of such an object. Adopting a phenomenological perspective, he suggested that it should be understood as "a purely intentional object."[70] Deferring the discussion on this topic,[71] we may for the moment recall another more common explanation: that which

67 This is not the case in the example under study here: in the preface to the *Köln Concert*'s authorized transcription (Edition Schott, 1990), Jarrett recommends using the recording as a "final-word reference."

68 See for instance Tomasz Trzcinski's version (https://www.youtube.com/watch?v=T_IW1wLZhzE), which had 3, 658, 917 views as of 15 April 2020. This version was criticized by Stéphane Gasparini, in "Le Köln Concert de Tomasz Trzcinski," in *Quand l'enregistrement change la musique*, ed. Alessandro Arbo and Pierre-Emmanuel Lephay (Paris: Hermann, 2017), 219–239.

69 This is the case of Valentin Lefèvre's version of Part I: https://www.youtube.com/watch?v=aPowHBj_gvY&list=PLWtfxqVrcN8WrLmGRAoci6FuzsYkis3XH.

70 "No real, individual object can be either such a variously indeterminate schema or a multiplicity of possibilities pertaining to that schema, which moreover are supposed to be embodied in performances realized in individual and real acts." Roman Ingarden, *The Work of Music and the Problem of Its Identity*, transl. Adam Czerniawski, ed. Jean G. Harrell (Houndmills: Macmillan, 1986), 152. On the ontological implications of the idea of a "purely intentional object" see Amie L. Thomasson, "Ingarden and the Ontology of Cultural Objects," in *Existence, Culture, Persons: The Ontology of Roman Ingarden*, ed. Arkadiusz Chrudzimski (Frankfurt: Ontos, 2005), 115–136.

71 See below, § 2.2, 36–38.

consists in describing such an object – from Richard Wollheim's seminal work[72] – as a "type," a structure or a rule that stipulates the properties that an occurrence – or "token" – must have to be considered as one of its concrete replicas or instances.[73] In a certain way, this condition does not particularly concern musical works: even in the case of perceiving a "mere" musical object (as a scale, a chord, an interval, etc.) we focus on something that is *beyond* the simple contingent reality of the sounds and that looks like a sort of type. An arpeggio that is executed, for example, could instantiate an arpeggio's type. However, the type we try to locate through the sounds we hear seems different. Usually it has different proportions and qualities. Although this difference may sometimes be significant, there is another that is even more important: such a type actually is characterized by a more extensive normativity, especially in the case of notated works. It is, in this case, a structural type whose parts are sonic types. If you consider the aesthetic properties of this sound structure, there are good reasons to say that it is not a "pure" sound structure (as radical Platonic philosophers think), but an "indicated structure," as Jerrold Levinson calls it, bringing attention to the fact that such a structure is "indicated" by someone (the composer) at a given time in order to be re-instantiated.[74] One might wonder what happens if such a structure cannot be traced back to a specific

72 Richard Wollheim, *Art and Its Objects. Second edition* (Cambridge: Cambridge University Press, 1980), 50.

73 Introduced by Charles Sanders Peirce and applied to artistic objects by Richard Wollheim in *Art and its Objects*, Cambridge: Cambridge University Press, 2005, 153–160, this distinction is used to separate descriptive concepts from the physical objects that instantiate them. More broadly, it allows us to grasp the relationship between the unity of a model and the multiplicity of the entities it may instantiate. For instance, "2" is a type that can be instantiated in multiple occurrences that may differ in a few respects (such as size, style) as long as they comply with the morphology defined by the model: 2222… Embraced (among others) in the radical Platonic approaches of Nicholas Wolterstorff, *Works and Worlds of Art*, Oxford: Clarendon, 1980, Peter Kivy, "Platonism in Music: A Kind of Defense," *Grazer Philosophische Studien* 19 (1983), 109–29, and Julian Dodd, *Works of Music: An Essay in Ontology*, Oxford: Oxford University Press, 2007, as well as in Jerrold Levinson's moderate Platonic approach (*Music, Art, and Metaphysics*, 64), and in Stephen Davies's Aristotelian approach (*Themes in the Philosophy of Music*, 67–68), "type theory" has become the "dominant view in the ontology of music" since the 1980s; see Matheson and Caplan, "Ontology," 38.

74 I will go into more detail about the difference between the platonic type and the indicated type in §2.3. For other arguments suggesting the inadequacy of the "type-token" model, pointing out in particular that improvisation does not lend itself to being described as the "token" of a pre-existing "type" or as a type of its own (whose existence would be actualized by a recording), see Clément, Canonne "Sur l'ontologie de l'improvisation," in *Ontologie musicale: perspectives et débats*, ed. Alessandro Arbo and Marcello Ruta, 285–297 (Paris: Hermann, 2014) and Bertinetto, "Paganini Does Not Repeat," 309–313.

creative individuality: a popular song, very often, is not attributable to a single composer. But this problem may not be crucial, to the extent that it might be sufficient to trace the origin of a musical structure back to a more widespread but nevertheless particular context of creation (a traditional Polish Christmas carol can be identified on the basis of its national origin even if we do not know who exactly wrote it). Anyway, it is this kind of structure that pre-exists performance that we focus our attention on, instead of focusing mainly on performance in itself.

Such conduct basically differentiates the perception of musical works from the perception of improvised music. It is true that this difference is not generally admitted by philosophers and theorists, and it is in fact sometimes small.[75] But it does remain important if we think of the way we categorize what we hear. Indeed, when listening to a jazz improvisation, often it is the belief that we are hearing something unique (unrepeatable) that plays an essential role. Other music can similarly be perceived as a contingent, unique and ephemeral event. Some musical cultures actually are *mainly* based on performance:[76] even if in improvisational practices harmonic and rhythmic structures are easily recognizable, they do not account for the core process of aesthetic detailing, which belongs to the performative act. As we listen to a musical work, we target *through* the performance (or *in* the performance) a pre-existing structure that was intended to be replayed or re-instantiated.

This is an important point; when one listens to a musical work, one needs not only some skills in order to recognise a sound structure, but also knowing, at least to an essential extent, that such a structure is supposed to re-emerge in multiple instances within a context of artistic production. This point becomes clearer if we think of cases where such knowledge is lacking. There can be two alternatives: first (A.1) a listener who does not have the knowledge to help them to place the object in a sufficiently targeted production context; second (A.2) a listener who does not have the general knowledge to help them know if what they are listening to (in the sounds) is a type, an artefact or a model performance created in a given artistic context. The second alternative will remain unlikely if we take Schoenberg's *Pierrot Lunaire* as an example and a conservatory student as the listener; but the situation is not always quite so

75 Examples of this will be analyzed in part 3.

76 According to Andrew Kania, "Works, Recordings, Performances: Classical, Rock, Jazz" in *Recorded Music. Philosophical and Critical Reflections*, ed. Mine Dogantan-Dack (London: Middlesex University Press, 2008), 12–15, such is the regulating principle of jazz, where the listening public tends to focus on performance documents in the recordings which, even if they incorporate materials recognizable as songs, are not in the strict sense performances of works.

straightforward. As we have seen, there are musical traditions that place great store on the improvisatory aspects – like jazz, or to be more precise, one of the more common ways it is practiced (and heard), or African polyrhythm or overtone singing in East Asia. A listener may quite legitimately ask in such cases if the aim is to uncover a work in the performance or if we are rather (or mainly) dealing with a performance art. In the same way, someone who listens to a dub recording[77] without knowing anything about the genre could take it to be a reduced or corrupted sound file (the voice is missing, too much reverb, etc.). These examples can lead us to hesitate in identifying the objects in question. Perhaps it is worth repeating that a musical happening, a jam session or other kinds of improvisation can have artistic value and be the origin of an artefact that works aesthetically; but they cannot claim to have the kind of normativity that we usually grant to musical works. These can be listened to again and again: they possess an identity that lasts over time and impose a rule to anyone looking to play them. This characterizes a national anthem, a nursery rhyme, a pop song or a Beethoven symphony – beyond the intrinsic value that we may attribute to them or the institutional settings where they will be reprised or appreciated in some form. This does not, however, characterize a Coleman solo or an Asian throat singing performance.

In short, an improvisation with a certain artistic value should undeniably be considered as a "work" in the broader sense of the term, but it cannot be called that in the more specific (and yet common) sense discussed here. To avoid any misunderstandings, David Davies has suggested calling improvisations "performance-work," in contrast to "work-performance."[78] This solution has the merit of clearly highlighting the difference between the two. To keep things straightforward, I will nevertheless continue to use the terms "improvisation" and "work" as equivalents to Davies's concepts.

Whether this would be easily accepted in musicology departments is far from certain. A musicologist analysing a Beethoven quartet will not readily admit that a nursery rhyme is equivalent in status to the masterpiece they are looking into. In turn, an ethnomusicologist will tend to avoid the word "work" when examining global musical practices or traditions. Yet, I do believe that this is a cogent option, in the sense that it allows us to account for two fundamental ways of conceiving and making music. This is not just a question of historical context and origins: our time, Beethoven's and other eras before it

77 See Rodolphe Weyl, "Entre œuvre phonographique et improvisation: le cas du dub," in *Quand l'enregistrement change la musique*, edited by Alessandro Arbo and Pierre-Emmanuel Lephay, 153–170 (Paris: Hermann, 2017).

78 David Davies, *Philosophy of the Performing Arts* (Chichester: Wiley – Blackwell, 2011), 18.

have all experienced the coexistence of musical units performed or improvised in more or less institutionalized artistic settings. The genuine difference lies in the presence of a more assertive normativity in the sound artefact or result: when we call upon the concept of work, we draw on the belief that we are listening to (or playing) is (more or less) in conformity with a sound structure *previously conceived* (or *presently conceived*, in some cases) *to be reproduced.* On the other hand, when we speak of improvisation, we are ready to acknowledge that what we are listening to, in addition to having been more or less planned or invented on the spot, manifests a *primarily performative nature.* In short, as Alessandro Bertinetto pointed out, an improvisation in the stricter sense "is always at work in the dimension of the present," it "lives and dies in the course of a single performance and cannot be reproduced."[79] The opposite is true of works; they express a normativity in the form of a prescription that makes a sound structure reproducible. This structure not only can but *must* be rendered and made audible. Such a result can be obtained in a variety of ways. The most common consists in writing instructions on a score that musicians will have to follow; in other contexts, a successful musical execution will be presented as an example; in yet others, musicians record a phonographic track that specific devices will be able to reproduce. This suggests a typology of the methods of fixing the trace;[80] I will come back to this point in the following parts.

Still, in the reality of music, the boundaries between improvisations and works are often blurred. There are works that contain improvised sections (e.g. cadenzas in concertos for solo instruments), and there are improvisations based on sometimes highly detailed instructions, whose normative value is recognised. There are improvisations that turn into works through the author's own efforts, using sometimes uncomplicated procedures. Still, it seems less appropriate to speak of a work wherever the performance involves no reference to a pre-established musical structure for the performer or listener.

79 Alessandro Bertinetto, *Eseguire l'inatteso. Ontologia della musica e improvvisazione* (Roma: Il glifo, 2016), 94.

80 In my view, the "trace" is not only what is left from a past act, but every imprint that prescribes or enables future acts. This broad, twofold sense of the notion is inspired by Derrida's philosophy, especially when he observes that the trace is the "origin of sense," or more precisely "the differance which opens appearance and signification"; Jacques Derrida, *Of Grammatology*, transl. Gayatri Chakravorty Spivak (Baltimore and London: The John Hopkins University Press, 1997), 65.

1.4 *Performances*

The version of the concept of work I have chosen here – a musical structure designed to be reproduced – allows us to expand the class of works beyond the confines of Western musical tradition, while carving a distinctive space outside of its scope for improvised music. As it happens, both works and improvisations have a very close relationship with what is called "performance" in music. This section thus examines the multiple meanings of this concept in greater detail to better understand its relationships with works and improvisations.

Upon first glance, what is referred to by the term "performance" does not seem to be as compromised (in an ethnocentric sense) as "work": undeniably, in most settings where music is found worldwide, it is related to a performative activity. However, this immediately raises a lexical challenge, as the term has rather different meanings in European languages. To convey its English meaning, a French speaker might have to use the words *exécution* or *interprétation* – in French, *performance* is rather used to refer to a feat or a person or machine's remarkable achievement in a given field. The problem with both of these terms is that they usually imply a pre-existing musical content (in verbal form, they can be applied to a song, a sonata, etc.). The term *création* could be used were it not itself extremely ambiguous, as it can refer both to performance and composition. To circumvent (if not avoid) these problems, musicological discourse in French should adopt the Anglicism "performance," whose meaning is broader than its French counterpart, as it includes all acts of execution, interpretation and creation, and is now largely used in the international musical language.

What exactly are we talking about when we talk of a "performance," and more specifically of a "musical performance," though? A dictionary would tell us that it comes from the old French word *performer*, a verb itself derived from the late Latin word *performare*, "to give shape." But what exactly is "shaped" in a performance? The Italian Treccani dictionary explains that the generic meaning is "the concrete realization of an activity, behavior or of a given situation."[81] We are thus invited to identify its outcome more than the action itself. However, when we speak of musical performance, both meanings are plausible: we speak of the musician's "great performance" (the "end product" of their action), but also about the action that the player is carrying out. In the first case, our interest is focused more on the actual sound event; in the second, it has more to do with a goal-oriented action (which is sometimes indicated by

81 "Performance," in *Vocabolario online Treccani*, http://www.treccani.it/vocabolario/performance/.

the concept of "conduct"[82]). The latter meaning has been developed by contemporary art;[83] but it is perhaps more common, when discussing music, to focus on the outcomes of the action.[84]

In everyday language, a "musical performance" refers to the action of a musician playing or singing. This meaning implies the presence of a human subject: a record player or radio can play music but they cannot give a musical performance (although they might be manipulated by someone for that purpose, as is the case in some of John Cage's pieces or in what a DJ might do during a rave party). This is clearly not a sufficient distinction, however. Think of the case of someone singing in the shower or informally practicing on their instrument: can we say that they are engaged in a musical performance? This does not seem right, insofar as such actions may reflect the simple desire to react to the water temperature by some sort of sensory pleasure or to familiarize oneself with one's instrument. What is missing? It is generally considered that a musical performance entails the intention to address an audience that is in a position to appreciate it (the word "audience," which could be seen as problematic in that it refers to a classic Western setting, can also be replaced by the more generic "someone").

A further question is whether someone needs to actually witness the action[85] or take part in it in one way or another (when the event in question is more of a ritual than a show). To assume such a constraint seems excessive today, especially considering everything that sound reproduction and broadcasting technologies have made possible. Of a musician singing or playing on a live radio program or in a Facebook Live video, one will readily say that they are giving a musical performance, regardless of the actual presence of an audience where they are playing, or in fact of whether anyone is actually listening or watching. Of course, the awareness of being watched or listened to by varying numbers of people may influence the musician's playing, but this influence is not a key factor in making this action a musical performance. What matters, on the other hand, is that such an action comes with the intention of

82 See François Delalande, "La gestique de Gould: éléments pour une sémiologie du geste musical," in *Glenn Gould Pluriel*, ed. Ghyslaine Guertin (Verdun: Louise Courteau, 1988), 85–111.

83 Tania Vladova, "Performance," in *Dictionnaire d'esthétique et de philosophie de l'art*, ed. Jacques Morizot and Roger Pouivet (2nd ed. Paris: Armand Colin, 2007), 354–355.

84 As does for example Peter Kivy, *Introduction to a Philosophy of Music* (Oxford: Clarendon Press, 1998), 205–206.

85 Cf. Stan Godlovitch, *Musical Performance. A Philosophical Study* (London and New York: Routledge, 1998), 49 and Paul Thom, *For an Audience: A Philosophy of the Performing Arts* (Philadelphia: Temple University Press, 1993), 193.

addressing someone in a position to appreciate it.[86] This makes performance an act or conduct that intentionally addresses listeners.[87]

Another potentially contentious point is the extension of the concept in question: when we say "performance," should we limit this to mean the actions produced directly by musicians on their instruments, or can we include all the activities related to the finalization of their products, in particular recordings? Basically, a recording is indeed a "musical gesture" (as Jacques Hains has written).[88] Nicholas Cook encourages us to take this idea even further:[89] given that today, the difference between on-stage and recorded performances is not always easy to tell apart and that recordings are not limited to merely playing the role of documenting a performance, then the work of recording producers and sound engineers should also be included in the notion of "performing" (and of performance), and thus recordings should explicitly be considered as performances of sorts, liable to constitute interpretations of works in their own right.

This idea – inspired by suggestions made by Aaron Ridley[90] and Glenn Gould[91] – is valid insofar as it attempts to take into account an activity that has become increasingly important thanks to advances in recording techniques in

86 As Kania, Andrew and Gracyk, Theodore, "Performances and Recordings," in *The Routledge Companion to Philosophy and Music*, ed. Andrew Kania and Theodore Gracyk (London and New York: Routledge, 2011), 81, have noted by observing that this argument could be extended to the production of some musical recordings.

87 For the most part, I use the definition proposed by Godlovitch, *Musical Performance*, 15–30. For a more extensive discussion on the specific nature of artistic performance, see David Davies, *Philosophy of the Performing Arts*, Chichester, West Sussex: John Wiley & Sons, 2011, 4–20. In a broader perspective, Christopher Small, *Musicking. The Meaning of Performing and Listening* (Middletown: Wesleyan University Press, 1998, 9) suggests considering musical performance as a complex system of relationships whose basis is "musicking," which includes not only the activity of musicians and listeners, but also "what the person is doing who takes the tickets at the door or the hefty men who shift the piano and the drums or the roadies who set up the instruments and carry out the sound checks or the cleaners who clean up after everyone else has gone." This holistic approach is fruitful when it comes to considering the meanings of a performance within its specific socio-cultural contexts, but seems redundant for the purposes of a definition.

88 Jacques Hains, "Du rouleau de cire au disque compact," in Jean-Jacques Nattiez (ed.), *Musiques: une encyclopédie pour le XXIe siècle. 1. Musiques du XXe siècle* (Paris: Actes Sud/ Cité de la musique, 2003), 934–935.

89 See Nicholas Cook, *Beyond the Score: Music as Performance* (Oxford: Oxford University Press, 2013), 358.

90 Aaron Ridley, *The Philosophy of Music. Theme and Variations* (Edinburgh: Edinburgh University Press, 2004), 111.

91 See Pierre-Emmanuel Lephay, "La prise de son et le mixage, éléments de l'interprétation: les exemples de Herbert von Karajan et Glenn Gould," in *Musique et enregistrement*, ed.

the second half of the twentieth century (not to mention the advent of digital technology). Such a widening of the concept's meaning may nevertheless raise other problems by leading us to conflate practices which, in the way the musical act is most commonly represented, remain distinct. We know very well that the final product of studio work is the result of cooperation between various people such as the producer, the sound engineer and, of course, the musician(s); and yet in layman's terms we tend to think that a "musical performance" only involves the action of musicians on their instruments, and not the actions of sound engineers labouring over their mixing desks. These roles are today generally thought of as being quite distinct.

In light of observations made in the previous section, the term "performance" here should be broken down into two main options: 1) the performance of a work or 2) a performance that has artistic value in itself.[92] In the former case, performance has artistic value insofar as it presents itself as the instantiation of a performed work; in the latter, it calls attention to itself (even though it might refer to a pre-existing structure). The issue may be further complicated when we consider the situation where the musicians perform in a recording studio: if a performance normally entails being given before an audience at a given time, does this mean we should distinguish it from a "studio performance"[93] or should we deny the studio version the status of a performance?[94] Be that as it may, it seems to us that it is in our interest to distinguish the studio product from the product of the performative act. At this juncture, I propose to introduce the term "work of performance" to refer to the former.[95] This category will enable us to better understand the transformation of the performative act into a product which, for its part, is intended to be lasting and re-identifiable, i.e. an object that we can classify, study or collect, as is brilliantly explained in Evan Eisenberg's book.[96]

Pierre-Henry Frangne and Hervé Lacombe (Rennes: Presses Universitaires de Rennes, 2014), 118–120.

92 This matches Davies's aforementioned distinction between "work-performance" and "performance-work."

93 Stephen Davies, *Musical Works and Performances. A Philosophical Exploration* (New York: Oxford University Press, 2001), 32.

94 Roger Pouivet, *Philosophie du rock. Une ontologie des artefacts et des enregistrements* (Paris: Presses Universitaires de France, 2010), 64–65.

95 Alessandro Arbo, "Qu'est-ce qu'un enregistrement musical(ement) véridique?," in *Musique et enregistrement* ed. Pierre-Henry Frangne and Hervé Lacombe (Rennes: Presses Universitaires de Rennes, 2014), 182–183. See below, 85.

96 Eisenberg, *The Recording Angel.*

1.5 *A Double-Sided Art*

In the musicological literature, relationships between the concepts of work and performance have often been conceived in terms of a priority granted to one or the other on principle. According to some musicologists, writing the history of music means first and foremost addressing works.[97] Until around twenty years ago, philosophers also mostly focused on works, treating performances mostly as more or less compliant, accurate or "authentic" interpretations of a work. This might appear to make sense if we take highbrow music from Beethoven and Schoenberg (and doubtless far beyond that), but far less so when dealing with a *khoomei* or a *katajjaq* performance or a jam session. As several scholars have explicitly pointed out, using the type/token model to study such phenomena leads to misunderstandings and ultimately further confuses things.[98] Indeed, these examples show that we would be wrong to generalize this paradigm and assume that as a rule performance comes *after* the works. On the contrary, as it has sometimes been argued, its foundational role should be recognised.

In his widely-read book, composer and musicologist Christopher Small argued that "most of the world's musicians [...] have no use for musical scores."[99] Based on the principle that "the fundamental nature and meaning of music lie not in objects, not in musical works at all, but in action, in what people do,"[100] we may soon come to the conclusion that "performance does not exist in order to present musical works, but rather, musical works exist in order to give performers something to perform."[101] Additionally, performance is a more universal and original way of working in music, an art that has presented itself in most civilizations and since time immemorial as a performative art. Scholars focusing on the centrality of practices and the variability of the meaning of works across historical time may even end up claiming that the concept of work is a sort of linguistic error, resulting from our tendency to reify our musical acts.[102] Taking a more ontological slant, Bertinetto suggests we consider them as "fictions" aimed at concealing "a real process of (dis)continuous and differential creative

97 This position is for instance supported by Carl Dahlhaus, *Foundations of Music History*, trans. J. B. Robinson (Cambridge and London: Cambridge University Press, 1983).

98 See Bertinetto, "Paganini Does Not Repeat."

99 Small, *Musicking*, 7.

100 Small, *Musicking*, 8.

101 Small, *Musicking*, 8.

102 Small, *Musicking*, 4.

(trans)formation."[103] This would make performance – or to be more precise, improvised performance – the only experiential reality in music.[104]

These arguments are based on seemingly convincing observations and/or conjectures. It is for instance quite likely that music began as a performative art. However, this assumption could be challenged on the grounds that when we look at ancient musical cultures, we are very often faced with pieces intended to be performed. One may also observe that ever since it has become possible to record sounds or reproduce them on some device, it has become perfectly conceivable to deal with music that implies no musical performance, or more radically yet, whose production did not involve any musical performance. This goes for electronic music, both in its highbrow and lowbrow iterations. In short, while we can very well conceive of a musical performance without works, we can just as well conceive of a musical work without performances. But what conclusions are we to draw from this?

Perhaps the following: while the relationship between works and performances can be established in terms of complementarity, this is not a necessary condition. Despite arguments that have sought to steer music towards either of those two poles, this art is characterized by an intrinsic ambivalence, being able to function equally as an *art of the trace* and as an *art of performance* (in the stricter sense). In other words, it is an art in which the performative act can equally be a way to render preexisting musical structures or the main (and sometimes) only object produced by the performer, on which our attention is focused. It is essential to take this ambivalence fully into account in order to make a systematic study of musical facts and acts.

The question that needs to be asked before making any attempt at valid knowledge-building in musicology could therefore be formulated as follows: does the music we are listening to or analysing mostly or mainly behave as an

103 Bertinetto, *Eseguire l'inatteso*, 8. This remark was later expanded by the author into the basis of a broader thesis on the improvisational nature of artistic practices; see Alessandro Bertinetto, "Improvisation and Ontology of Art," *Rivista di Estetica* 73 (2020), 10–29.

104 For other (more moderate) fictionalist theses about musical work, see Andrew Kania, "The Methodology of Musical Ontology: Descriptivism and Its Implications," and Anton Killin, "Fictionalism about Musical Works," *Canadian Journal of Philosophy* 48 (2017), 266–91. More nihilistic is Ross Cameron's position, according to which, although the phrase "there are musical works" is true, actually there are no musical works; see Ross Cameron, "There Are No Things That Are Musical Works," *British Journal of Aesthetics* 48, N. 3 (2008), 295–314. Cameron's thesis has been criticised by Roger Pouivet, who opposed it by means of a solid aesthetic realism: Roger Pouivet, "Les œuvres musicales existent-elles? Un dialogue ontologique," in *Ontologie musicale: perspectives et débat*, ed. Alessandro Arbo and Marcello Ruta (Paris: Hermann, 2014), 13–32.

art of the trace or as an art of performance? Finding a convincing answer to this question through a priori reasoning (if the latter can even be done properly) seems implausible; we need to look at the contexts in which or for which a given music has been conceived. This involves establishing if, in the expectations of those who play, sing, listen or maybe even dance, we can identify a reference to a (more or less complex) sound structure with a normative value. A fiddler taking a stab at an Irish jig, a band covering a Bob Dylan song, and a pianist interpreting a Brahms *Intermezzo* are certainly responding to diverse constraints: yet, they are all faced with the task of rendering features of a pre-existing musical unit that is supposed to last over time and will therefore have to be highlighted in their performances in one way or another.[105] This is not the case of musicians who "perform" a free improvisation. Obviously, this does not mean that the act of improvising is entirely free of any sort of constraint, but that it manifests another degree of normativity: the musician has to work with musical elements (gestures, cadences, ways of singing, phrases) that a listener may consider as more or less familiar or specific to a given culture. These elements establish a framework for action but do not make a work in themselves.

Still, even if we admit that there are situations that can be described according to the aforementioned categories, there are others that are unlikely to fit within such a handy categorization. Take a work such as Karlheinz Stockhausen's *Klavierstück XI* (1956). The composer requires the pianist to create the work's structure based on a series of finely notated musical fragments: does that still make it mostly a work, or an improvisation? Another example: when performing a standard from the *Real Book*, such as "You Don't Know What Love Is,"[106] a musician is expected both to improvise and to make the listener recognize a pre-existing sound structure. These two cases go a long way towards suggesting just how spurious any attempt at distinguishing works and performances can get.

In fact, in my opinion, they especially point to the pertinence, or even the need of never losing sight of the tension or categorial opposition between conceptions of music intrinsically linked to the concepts of, respectively, work and performance. Stockhausen's work gets a mention at the beginning of Umberto

105 It should be noted that the idea of lasting over time does not exclude every kind of change: like a person who continues to be the same person and changes (because he or she gets older) even a painting or an electronic work can last and change, if only because the physical support deteriorates.

106 Written by Don Raye (lyrics) and Gene de Paul (music) for the Abbott and Costello picture *Keep 'Em Flying* (1941).

Eco's famous book *The Open Work*,[107] exemplifying the "special" poetics of works that involve a component of indeterminacy. Such a strategy arguably reflects the explicit intention to open up the concept of what a work is, and even, one might say, to reintroduce performance *into* the work. This means that, to understand Stockhausen's *Klavierstuck XI*, a fine understanding of the "work" category is required, with its advantages and limitations (including the fact that it sometimes seems to be too frozen in time).

Consider now a jazz musician's work on a standard. On the one hand, we have a pre-existing musical structure that manifests a clear normativity: if you launch into "You Don't Know What Love Is," the listener must be able to recognize the melodic profile or the harmonic structure of that song in particular, not another. However, it might seem reductive to consider the performances of this popular song by Chet Baker, John Coltrane or Lennie Tristano as mere interpretations of that work, but for what reasons? The fact is that, in jazz, higher artistic value is placed on the performer's ability not to render the connotations of a pre-existing musical structure, but rather to adapt it, to modify it, to harmonize it or to even to carve an original path *based on it*. As Andrew Kania noted,[108] in the jazz tradition the primary focus of appreciation is on performances: the attention of an expert listener will focus more on them than on the trace they are supposed to leave behind. This does not mean that a standard cannot be considered as a work.[109] It is indeed a work that leaves a lot of leeway to performers: an ontologically "thin" work, to use a category by Stephen Davies.[110] But this should not prevent us from recognising, as Davies himself does,[111] that a performance appears as an improvisation inspired by this standard (it comes from or "after it"), and can therefore manifest aesthetic and ontological properties that substantially differ from those of the song from which it was inspired. Lennie Tristano's version, for instance, is evidently merely the pretext or starting point of a harmonic and virtuosic journey that is mostly about the performance itself. Indeed, it is the way in which such a trace "operates" – or how it is "activated," to use Goodman's term – that ends up altering its status: in jazz, the characteristics of improvisation and performance are expected to prevail over those of the work, which becomes a simple

107 Umberto Eco, *The Open Work*, trans. Anna Cancogni (Cambridge, Massachusetts: Harvard University Press, 1989), 1.

108 See Andrew Kania, "All Play and No Works," *The Journal of Aesthetics and Art Criticism* 69, n. 4 (2011), 398.

109 See Julian Dodd, "Upholding Standards: A Realist Ontology of Standard Form Jazz," *The Journal of Aesthetics and Art Criticism* 72, n. 3 (2014), 277–290.

110 S. Davies, *Musical Works and Performances*, 20.

111 S. Davies, *Musical Works and Performances*, 16–17.

trace that the improvising musician may draw from (or refer to). The focus of attention is clearly placed on the improviser's work – which puts emphasis on the meaning of music as a performative art rather than as an art of the trace.

Evidently, the aforementioned cases – and others – cannot be considered uniformly. Therein precisely lies at least one aspect of their artistic value: they highlight the coexistence and occasional tension between the normativity of the "work" category and a performativity that cannot always be reduced to the performance of a work.

1.6 *Conclusions*

After having highlighted the value of a certain meaning given to the concepts of "work," "improvisation" and "performance," I have gone on to discuss the relationships among them. I have shown that it is better to refrain from establishing a hierarchy between these concepts or principles, so that music can retain its double meaning as an art of performance and an art of the trace. As this double-sided status causes terminological and conceptual ambiguity, it should be fully reckoned with by anyone aspiring to producing valid knowledge of musical facts. The ability to discern whether a phenomenon mainly reflects the intention to render a pre-existing musical structure or to produce a performance with intrinsic value will provide a more solid foundation on which to make descriptions, explanations and judgments about the facts or events we examine. An awareness of these differences is a key pre-requisite to the study of both paradigmatic cases and more ambiguous and liminal ones.

2 Musical Ontology: An Overview

2.1 *Introduction*

This second part will clarify what musical works consist of, that is to say, how their identity is defined and how their aesthetic functioning is expressed. In other words, I will continue the reflection from an ontological perspective. Let us therefore begin by clarifying how I will conceive the term "ontology" and the kind of research to which it refers.

In musical ontology, we can distinguish some primary issues. One is to wonder if certain things we are talking about actually exist or if they are only apparent beings, due to an error of language or thought ("do musical works really exist?"[112]). Another one is to wonder how the things we consider to exist

112 See for exemple Roger Pouivet's criticism of Ross Cameron's nihilist view: Pouivet, "Les œuvres musicales existent-elles? Un dialogue ontologique," 17–32.

actually exist ("what kind of thing is a musical work?"[113]). A third one is to ask what are the conditions of identity for something to be considered as existing in a certain way ("how can we identify a musical work in something?").[114] Scholars have recently debated the priority of one or another of these issues with respect to the definition of aesthetic problems relating to musical works: according to some, in order to evaluate the way in which musical works are presented or performed, we need to begin by knowing if and how they exist or what kind of things they are;[115] according to others, such knowledge is useless when it comes to evaluating musical performances.[116] While this is outside the scope of this essay, it is nevertheless appropriate to clarify my position.

My assumption, expressed since the introduction (and elsewhere argued[117]), is that the awareness of how musical entities exist is useful for addressing the problems that have traditionally been considered of aesthetic relevance – including the perception and evaluation of musical works. At the same time, such an awareness does not constitute a necessary logical premise of the aesthetic discourse.[118] I will deal with ontological issues by making reference mainly to the second and the third of the issues mentioned above, i.e. modality and identity. As philosophically relevant as it may be, the question of whether musical works really exist is not central to our discussion. We have already observed that in most of the world's cultures, there is the belief that music comprises performative acts, but also songs, hymns, dances, symphonies and other such "things": we think that, even if someone were to succeed with a strongly revisionist, nominalist or nihilist approach, that such things are nothing more than names, we would still continue to deal with them and to consider them in a certain way as existing – even if, at the same time, one of the most shared intuitions will lead us to recognise that they cannot exist

113 This is what Andrew Kania has called the "fundamentalist debate." See Kania, "The Philosophy of Music," §2.1.

114 Christopher Bartel, "Music Without Metaphysics?," 384–385, has called this issue the "identity debate," in order to clearly distinguish it from the fundamentalist debate. More generally this kind of research is considered by Kania, "The Philosophy of Music," §2.1, as "Higher-level Ontological Issues."

115 Andrew Kania, "New Waves in Musical Ontology," in *New Waves in Aesthetics*, ed. Kathleen Stock and Katherine Thomson-Jones (New York: Palgrave Macmillan, 2008), 33–34.

116 The most radical position in this regard has probably been taken by Ridley, "Against Musical Ontology."

117 Alessandro Arbo, "Jugement esthétique et ontologie musicale," *International Review of Aesthetics and Sociology of Music* 45, n. 1 (2014), 3–19.

118 In this regard we agree with the "weakened" versions of the priority of ontology defended by Bartel, "Music Without Metaphysics?" and Giombini, *Musical Ontology. A Guide for the Perplexed.*

as *physical* things.[119] I will start from this common-sense assumption – what in other words we could call a "naive realistic hypothesis" about the existence of musical works – and clarify such a presumed reality; in other words, how such particular "things," exist and how we can correctly identify them. The first of these issues will be dealt with in a more general way in this second part and in a more detailed way in the third, which will also deal with identity issues. In pursuing these aims, I will consider some classical paradigms of musical ontology, in particular those that refer to the type/token couple and those that refer to the notion of artistic artefact. My overview is not exhaustive and is limited to a few key models.[120]

2.2 *The Musical Work as an Intentional Object*

As we have already mentioned, Roman Ingarden was probably the first to develop a complete philosophical theory on musical works. In his essay published in the 1950s, but first written in the late 1920s, he argues that musical works are linked to our imaginative activity and have their own mode of existence. In other words, they manifest an ontological peculiarity that is worth examining. Because they do not coincide either with the score or any of its performances (insofar as these can be considered original, as they may have been realized by the composer himself[121]), they cannot in fact be considered as "real objects." Ingarden's idea is the following: if musical works "spring from the creative act of the composer" and have their "ontic base" (*Seinsfundement*) "directly in the score," their very nature is that of a "purely intentional object."[122] This ontological particularity characterises, in Ingarden's perspective, not only musical works but all cultural objects: a kind of objects that are at the same time mind-dependent and "'transcendent' with respect to [...] all conscious acts."[123] Only such a nature could explain that it is "one and the same object, which endures in historical time but undergoes gradual change."[124]

But what would be the subject of intentional acts that ensure the slow transformation in historical time of this "one and the same object"? In the final part

119 As stressed by Robert Stecker, "Methodological Questions about the Ontology of Music," *Journal of Aesthetics and Art Criticism* 67 (2009): 376.

120 More complete overviews of the multiple models for explaining musical works can be found in the articles and books mentioned in note 1 of the introduction.

121 Ingarden, *The Work of Music and the Problem of Its Identity*, 148.

122 Ingarden, *The Work of Music and the Problem of Its Identity*, 117.

123 Roman Ingarden, *The Literary Work of Art*, transl. George G. Grabowicz (Evanston, Illinois: Northwestern University Press, 1973), 118; see Thomasson, "Ingarden and the Ontology of Cultural Objects," 120–121.

124 Ingarden, *The Work of Music and the Problem of Its Identity*, 151.

of his essay, Ingarden directs our attention to "an intersubjective aesthetic object," an intentional correlate of a "debate among experts and laymen."[125] In the end, Ingarden acknowledges, it can be considered a kind of "social object"[126] that has the particularity of deriving its existence intentionally from "creative acts, instructions within the score" and "the listeners' conjectures"; in short, an object that exists "heteronomously" and whose properties are "ultimately dependent upon the opinions we hold of them."[127]

This explanation opens up an interesting line of enquiry, even if its limits are quite clear. First of all, it seems to refer to one and only one type of work: the one based on a score that is likely to allow us to re-instantiate the work. Ingarden does in fact accept that we can nowadays resort to less "imperfect" means of indicating the intended sounds than musical notation, such as a tape-recording.[128] But he rejects this possibility for several reasons: first of all, if the recorded performance is made by the composer himself, it will not necessarily be the best one imaginable, as long as we accept that composers are not always the best interpreters of their own works; the use of a talented performer will not guarantee the perfect identity of the object, as long as he might introduce personal deviations; the reproduction equipment, finally, might not be up to the standard desired by the composer.[129] These limitations show us that Ingarden primarily thinks of the musical recording as a documentary-recording of a (singular) performance of the work. However, as we have already observed, and as we will develop in the third part, this option hardly corresponds to all the functions of a musical recording. As for works of an orally-transmitted nature, they would be, in his view, literally "unfounded" objects (or apparent objects lacking an ontic base).

There is also another, more general difficulty: Ingarden's approach is based on an idea of intentionality which, because of its subjective and mental dimension, is nevertheless a form of derealization. A musical work does not exist in a strong sense of the word: it "quasi-exists," or it exists only to the extent that we experience it. But would intentionality really be capable of generating objects that endure in historical time? Can we really consider the way a musical work is made is really so detached from the outside world and ontologically dependent on the opinions of its listeners? If this is the case, we would like to know a little more about those who make it so: would it be the experts or the listeners

125 Ingarden, *The Work of Music and the Problem of Its Identity*, 154.
126 Ingarden, *The Work of Music and the Problem of Its Identity*, 154.
127 Ingarden, *The Work of Music and the Problem of Its Identity*, 155.
128 Ingarden, *The Work of Music and the Problem of Its Identity*, 117.
129 Ingarden, *The Work of Music and the Problem of Its Identity*, 117–118.

who experience it and form their own opinions? If this is the case, it seems unlikely that this group could share a single opinion. But what about multiple and conflicting opinions? Doesn't such a divergence risk eliminating the identity of what should be recognised as *one and the same* work?

2.3 *Nominalism and Type/Token Theory*

As shown by many theoretical models that have flourished in analytical philosophy from the 1950s and 1960s until today, there are several ways out of this impasse. The first way is to refute the existence of something as an abstract or intentional object, and to admit only particular concrete entities. In Goodman's view, the musical work is no longer an individual entity (real or intentional), but a "compliance-class" that is able to group a set of performances starting from a rule (consisting of the score).[130] What ensures the unity of the work in historical time is therefore the full normativity of a notational system. The latter ensures respect for the principle of "disjointness of the characters";[131] it makes music an eminently "allographic" art; that is to say, an art in which the main criterion for identifying works is "ortographic."

This conception of musical works has had an extraordinary influence on the analytical aesthetic and ontological debate and has been the subject of much debate. Without entering into the details of these discussions, I will limit the argument to a summary of its main merits and difficulties and will deepen the issue relating to this kind of normativity in the next part.

Goodman's view shows, in addition to a great logical coherence of reasoning, an extreme economy on an ontological level: he succeeds in explaining reality by merely admitting the existence of concrete and individual entities. Nevertheless, the intent to eliminate the "work" as an entity and considering it instead as a class of performances appears counterintuitive. Furthermore, this theory subscribes to an implicit and unjustified privilege of the notation,[132] underestimating or simply ignoring (like in Ingarden's approach) oral and phonographic works. It gives rise, moreover, to some uncomfortable paradoxes. Peter Kivy has highlighted some of them:[133] if we conceive musical works as classes of performances, then we should recognise that such classes are bound to remain incomplete (since they should include not only performances that have already taken place, but future performances). We should also draw the

130 Goodman, *Languages of Arts*, 210: "In music, the work is the class of performances compliant with a character."

131 Goodman, *Languages of Arts*, 133.

132 As stressed by Jean Molino, *Le singe musicien. Essais de sémiologie et d'anthropologie de la musique* (Arles: Actes Sud, 2009), 387.

133 Peter Kivy, *Introduction to a Philosophy of Music*, 208.

conclusion that, at the moment when a composer completes the score of one of his works, it does not yet exist – and the same could be said of all the works that remain unperformed. And again: if all the performances of a work (at least all those produced up to a given moment) were to be dull or inexpressive, would we have the right to say that the work in itself is inexpressive?

Further theories have tried to solve these problems by considering the work as a "fusion" of performances[134] or a "continuant" depending on performances.[135] The point is to find a way to "save" the unity of the work in the face of its multiple performances. But the most classic alternative solution to Goodmanian nominalism was formulated by Platonism.[136] This term should not mislead us: if its arguments seem to resurrect a form of Platonism, its main source of inspiration is not Plato's work but, as we have already pointed out above,[137] Peirce's "type/token" theory. In short, works should be considered as "types" whose ontological feature consists precisely in being *real* without being *physical*. This implies that, like any abstract or ideal entity, musical works exist, fundamentally, outside space and time:[138] they do not begin to exist, contrary to a common opinion, via an act of creation, and do not cease to exist. Nor, Kivy adds, can they interact with our world, because they are "causally inert."[139] Such then would be the nature of musical works; a nature that should in principle be considered as being clearly distinct from that of performances (which, for their part, are tokens situated in time and space).

If the distinction between works and performances – and more particularly between what presents itself as an object (ideal or abstract) and what, in the space-time continuum, presents itself as an event[140] – is common, the

134 See Caplan, Ben and Carl Matheson, "Defending Musical Perdurantism," *British Journal of Aesthetics* 46 (2006), 59–69.

135 Guy Rohrbaugh, "Artworks as Historical Individuals," *European Journal of Philosophy* 11 (2003), 177–205. For a quick look at these (and several others) perspectives, see Davies, "Works of Music: Approaches to the Ontology of Music from Analytic Philosophy," 11–12.

136 Peter Kivy, "Platonism in Music: A Kind of Defense," *Grazer Philosophische Studien* 19 (1983), 109–29; Julian, Dodd, *Works of Music: An Essay in Ontology* (Oxford: Oxford University Press, 2007).

137 See above §1.2.

138 Dodd, *Works of Music*, 42–43; Kivy, *Introduction*, 211.

139 Kivy, *Introduction*, 211.

140 Indeed, even though the ontological debate has tried to explain in what sense musical works can be recognised as objects that endure over time by making them mental objects, types, abstract structures or artefactual entities, it has above all emphasised the event-driven nature of performances. Some perspectives have even gone so far as to recognise that the works themselves can be thought of as a sort of event. This is the case in the thesis put forward by Gregory Currie (*An Ontology of Art*, London: Macmillan, 1989), in which every art form (not only performance-based, but also the visual or plastic arts, for

fact of marking their difference in nature makes this conception highly (and consciously) revisionist. Indeed, normally we tend to think of musical works as human productions; as something that we can sometimes unfortunately lose or destroy (as happened with some of Monteverdi's operas, for example); and, finally, as an entity that interacts well with our world, in time (chronological and historical) and space (physical and geographical). We need only think of the extent to which a single work can sometimes make us change our ways of thinking about composition or listening (for example, works such as Schoenberg's *Pierrot lunaire*, Stravinsky's *Le Sacre du printemps*, or Gérard Grisey's *Les espaces acoustiques*).

In the face of these objections (and many others), Kivy gradually developed a series of precise and detailed arguments. We will limit ourselves here to mentioning those that he most frequently put forward: to those who questioned the existence of ideal entities outside of time and physical space, he simply recalled that, insofar as mathematics exists and that we continue to do mathematics, such realities do in fact exist.[141] As for the opinion that a work must inevitably be the result of an act of creation, Kivy replied that the very idea of creation (and even more so the idea of an individually connoted creation) is not as universal as one might think at first glance; a composer thus often looks

example) should be considered as "action types," because they are constituted by the action of the person who discovers a structure – whose value remains universal – at a given moment. Nevertheless, even if it seems reasonable to say that the appreciation and/or the understanding of a work and/or a performance have much to gain from knowing the steps that the composer and/or performer have adopted to overcome the technical and artistic problems with which they have been confronted, it would be too simplistic to make the essential part of our appreciation coincide with this aspect: if that were the case, we could then say that very few people would be able to appreciate musical works (and works of art in general). Moreover, in Currie's theory, the idea of an "action type," which supports a form of Platonic essentialism, ends up making performances of occurrences of occurrences – a solution that is both complicated and counterintuitive; see Roger Pouivet, *L'ontologie de l'œuvre d'art: une introduction*, (Paris: Vrin, 2010), 52. David Davies' perspective (*Art as Performance*, Oxford: Blackwell, 2004) avoids this multiplication of entities: if any artistic outcome can be understood in terms of action (i.e. as a process and not as a stable entity), it would be better to think of works as well as performances as being *tokens* rather than as *types*. This is a well-founded theory; we nevertheless wonder how useful it is to conflate the outcome of creative action with the action. Is there really any use in saying that when we listen to Handel's *Messiah* we are listening to the action of the musicians and the action of Handel as the composer of the *Messiah*? After all, in our ordinary discussions, works are presented to us as units distinct from the actions that are supposed to produce or instantiate them. In our opinion, we should follow the common pre-theoretical sense and continue to distinguish the more "stable" character of works from the (eminently) event-driven nature of performances.

141 Kivy, *Introduction to a Philosophy of Music*, 211.

for sound structures that, on closer inspection, are still there, or have always been there, just like the mathematical laws or rules of geometry that have been discovered – and not created or invented – by scientists.[142]

Both in the formulation of its ideas and in its responses to its detractors, Platonism has proven to be anchored to a solid and coherent form of realism. At the same time, however, this view appears to be counterintuitive and leaves more than one question open. If every composer discovers sound structures that are already there, why were certain structures discovered in Bach's time rather than in Brahms' or our own? If what matters are the properties of the sound structure,[143] why, in most musical cultures, did we end up paying so much attention to contextual properties? Can the identification of the aesthetic properties of a work really disregard the fact that it is an original composition, an arrangement of a previous composition, a (simple) exercise in style, a piece for didactic purposes, a traditional song or an improvisation?

Starting from the assumption that musical works, like works of art in general, "have a number of important aesthetic and artistic properties that they could not have were they pure structures existing atemporally, with no essential links to creative artists, preceding art-works, preceding artistic movement, and more generally, surrounding cultural environments,"[144] Jerrold Levinson has developed a model that largely answers these questions. His main idea is that musical works are "impure indicated structures"; that is, in his words, they are a kind of semi-abstract entity, "the result of the interaction between a person and an entirely abstract structure, such as a sequence or a series of words or notes."[145] Where the act of indication ensures that the sound structure is embedded in a system of relations and a context in which it assumes artistic meaning and value. This idea implies an important presupposition: in order to appreciate the aesthetic properties of musical works, the listener must have some appropriate capacities and categories.[146] This explains why the imitation of a Bach chorale, in so far as it can be acoustically indistinguishable from its model, does not have the same aesthetic properties as its model would have for an informed listener.

---

142 These arguments have been the subject of much discussion and robust criticism, particularly from Jerrold Levinson (see Levinson, *Music, Art, and Metaphysics*, 215–231).

143 Indeed this perspective has sometimes been referred to as "sonicism."

144 Levinson, *Musical Concerns*, 46.

145 Levinson, *Musical Concerns*, 46.

146 Levinson argues this contextualist principle (based on the arguments of C. Stevenson, W. E. Kennick and K. Walton), on his first essay "What a Musical Work Is" (1980), republished in *Music, Arts, and Metaphysics. Essays in Philosophical Aesthetics* (Oxford: Oxford University Press, 2011), 69.

It should be stressed that, from this standpoint, what characterises the act of "artistic indication" in relation to the act of "simple indication" is the intention to "leave a mark"[147] likely to subsist beyond the transitory act: just like a poet, a composer indicates, at a given moment in history, the words or notes that will one day have to be recreated in order to re-instantiate the linguistic or sonic structure to which he has directed our attention. We would also point out that such an act is accompanied by a kind of normative implementation: when Chopin indicates the notes of the mazurka he is composing, Levinson observes,

> What he establishes is a *rule*, a *norm*, a miniature *practice*, whereby pianists play a piece *by Chopin* and not just any piece of music when they play *that* sequence of notes chosen by Chopin, and do so precisely *because* that sequence was chosen by Chopin. That's what makes the Mazurka in A minor exist *as* a work by Chopin. To indicate, as a composer, a particular sequence of notes consists precisely in establishing a rule to reproduce the sounds in a certain way following the indications of a particular, historically situated mind. And it is as such an indicated structure that we can identify a classical musical work.[148]

The advantage of this explanation is that it provides a better account than the radical Platonic view of how musical works exist. Without renouncing the distinction between their nature and that of physical objects, it safeguards their objective and real character, while at the same time rooting them in a music-historical context. Indeed, it seems fair to say that the works of the Classical-Romantic tradition that have resulted from an act of composition, have aesthetic properties that do not depend exclusively on the sound structure (or the sound structure itself) but on the fact that it was chosen and precisely indicated by someone who had an explicit artistic intention at a given moment.

It should also be remembered that the "impurity" of the sound structure that may allow the identification of the work depends, in Levinson's theory, not only on the fact that the notes have been indicated by someone at a given moment, but also on the fact that it is a structure conceived in order to be played, i.e. linked to the implementation of some specific means of sound production.[149] In other words, a Chopin Mazurka played by a bagpipe or by a

147 Levinson, *Musical Concerns*, 49.
148 Levinson, *Musical Concerns*, 50.
149 Levinson, *Musical Concerns*, 78.

computer that perfectly imitates the sounds of a piano would not be identified as Chopin's work, since it is explicitly designed to be performed on a piano by a real musician. This second condition also seems to us to be acceptable, but with one caveat: it is valid only for a particular class of musical works, such as the score-based works of the Classical-Romantic tradition extending up to part of contemporary production. More generally, as Kivy rightly pointed out, we can consider that the attitude of composers has changed over the centuries and in different contexts:[150] in the Baroque period it is certainly not rare to find compositions that can be played equally well by a violin, an oboe or a flute (instruments that can play in the same register, but whose timbre and technical possibilities are very different).

Levinson's theory (likes Kivy's and Goodman's) was designed to explain score-based works (the standard examples are Beethoven's *Fifth Symphony* and, by the same composer, the *Quintet* for piano and winds in E-flat, op. 16) and their relation to the multiple performances that are supposed to embody them. It remains to be seen whether such an explanation could also apply to the musical structures that exist in oral cultures. As far as they are concerned, one should take into account the fact that their origin is not so easily identifiable (the composer – who, in fact, is most often a composer-performer – is often anonymous, unknown, or may coincide with several people who lived at different times); moreover, in an oral culture, the act of indication is done by example, that is to say, via a performative act, and not through notation, and while this act may direct us towards a certain family of instruments, it is rare for a specific instrument to be explicitly indicated for the piece (even if it may be implicit, as perhaps in the case of the *oud* in Tunisian music, the *duduk* for an Armenian melody, etc.). This theoretical model could therefore only be adapted at the cost of easing the conditions that characterize the act of indication (which, as we shall see in the next part, changes the situation). It also remains to be seen, finally, whether this model allows us to explain what a pop musician carries out when they produce their music in a studio; once again, this is a form of indication, which nevertheless calls for a completely different system of capturing and transmitting the trace: the (implicit) norm that accompanies such an indication would then no longer reside in the fact of executing the notes in a certain way, but rather in decoding and correctly reproducing the trace encoded on the medium.

150 Kivy, *Introduction*, 216–217.

We will retain from Levinson's theory the (central) idea that musical works are not entirely abstract types:[151] sound structures are somehow "embodied" and linked to a certain production context. Moreover, it seems equally important to us to take into account the conditions of their reception. In other words, it is not only a question of considering what the artist intended to indicate, but what the musicians and listeners are supposed to know or understand from what the composer has indicated. When a composer writes "Allegro," they assume that a musician knows how to put such an indication into action. This does not prevent the composer from introducing original (such as Mozart's "Allegro aperto"[152]) or extravagant (such as Satie's "Ouvrez la tête"[153]) variants; but these variants are likely to remain intelligible in relation to a base of categories and terms of reference that are presumably shared by the musicians and listeners of the composer's time and context. What the idea of "indicated structure" seems to ultimately bring out is not only the richness of the properties of a musical work (properties that cannot be reduced to its sound or perceptive properties) but also the complexity of the network of relations in which an act of indication can really function.

2.4 *Heterotropic Intentionality*

Both Ingarden's and Levinson's perspectives emphasize that the identification of a musical work derives from a necessary consideration of its music-historical contexts. In the final part of his essay, Ingarden thus encourages us to address an object whose nature is essentially "social." But what exactly do we mean by this?

At first glance, asserting that a musical work is a social object – or more precisely a *socially constructed* object, as in the examples we have just mentioned – does not seem to add much to our thinking. As Stephen Davies has observed,[154] we must bear in mind that many other human entities and practices are constructed in the same way: from baseball to book clubs, Kalashnikovs, etc., in short to any object concerned or affected in one way or another by culture, including certain natural objects. To see if this premise can help us, we must

151 An idea which has been, let us recall, vigorously criticized by Kivy, *Introduction to a Philosophy of Music*, 222. Other aspects of Levinson's theory have been the subject of a detailed discussion which we will not enter into here as it is beyond the scope of our subject. See note n. 2 of the article in which Levinson himself replied to his interlocutors, paying particular attention to the objections of Kivy (216–249), David Pearce (249–259), and James Anderson (259–263).

152 *Violin Concerto* in A k219 and Piano Concerto in B♭ k238.

153 "Think right!," *Gnossienne n. 3* (1890), Partition Salabert, 1913.

154 Stephen Davies, "Are musical works socially constructed kinds?," 1.

try to understand first what distinguishes social objects from other types of objects and second, what advantage is there to know that a musical work – or more generally all kinds of musical objects – belongs to the class of social objects.

John Searle, who in the 1990s authored one of the most developed theories on the constitution of social reality,[155] invites us to start from a general principle, the "assignment of function." It can be formulated simply as follows: "X counts as Y in C." For example: a piece of paper becomes a banknote with purchasing power in a given context.[156] Such an assignment would characterize our way of constituting the reality of social objects on physical objects. However, in order for this formula to work, we are invited to clarify the notion of intentionality: this is not a question of individual intentionality but of a specific "collective intentionality" (CI).[157]

Such an idea seems easily applicable to the situation at hand. A musical work would be a sound structure (X) that is counted as a work (Y) in a certain cultural, or more generally relational and human context (C), in which we can observe the presence of a collective intentionality (CI). This option, however, would immediately lead us to ask the following (as in part we have already done in the comments from Ingarden's perspective): what is the "subject" of such intentionality? Where is it? Can we possibly consider it as a kind of biologically inherited faculty? This idea would certainly allow us to avoid the pitfall of idealism but it would prove to be powerless to explain what it should be most attached to, namely cultural variations.[158] Moreover, we should not believe that all our social acts are so dependent on this kind of intentionality. If, by this term, we mean the intentionality of subjects who share a certain mental state or collective act, we should infer that it constitutes a special case: for example, that of musicians who play or improvise together, and who can all be considered in the same way as agents.[159] But it is apparently not the same

155 John Searle, *The Construction of Social Reality* (New York: Free Press, 1995).

156 "Bills issued by the Bureau of Engraving and Printing (X) count as money (Y) in the United States (C)"; Searle, *The Construction of Social Reality*, 28.

157 Searle, *The Construction of Social Reality*, 23–26. The premises of the idea of collective intentionality are present under other labels in the works of Emile Durkheim, Max Weber, Max Scheler; see Schweikard, David P. and Hans Bernhard Schmid, "Collective Intentionality," *The Stanford Encyclopedia of Philosophy*, Winter 2020 Edition, ed. Edward N. Zalta, URL: https://plato.stanford.edu/archives/win2020/entries/collective-intentionality/.

158 This and many other questions were raised during the debate following the publication of Searle's book. See Joshua Rust, *John Searle and The Construction of Social Reality* (London and New York: Continuum, 2006).

159 See Alfred Schütz, "Making Music Together. A Study in Social Relationship," *Social Research* 18, 1/4 (1951), 76–97.

when I promise something to someone: this someone is then the counterpart in the accomplishment of the social act, but our roles are different.

At this juncture it would be worthwhile to focus on the intentionality of social acts. This is subject to an intrinsic constraint: it *involves at least two subjects*. In technical terms, it is a "heterotropic" intentionality.[160] Heterotropism means that *social entities, while dependent on subjects, are not subjective*. This principle gives rise to a presupposition: in order for another person to constitute the counterpart of a social act of which I am the bearer, I must not only be able to externalize my act, but also *such an act must be recorded somewhere*. Imagine a promise between two persons who, because of an illness or an accident, both lose their memory: would this promise still exist? The situation is obviously different if such an act was recorded in some form of memory: a sheet of paper, a magnetic tape, a digital file, or the memory of some witness or other.

In his treatise *Documentalità* (2009),[161] Maurizio Ferraris showed the extent to which a recording is responsible for the constitution of any social object. In other words, a social object would be constituted – for the most part – by a registered act. This idea, which to some extent represents an original reinterpretation of a principle formulated by the phenomenologist and legal philosopher Adolf Reinach,[162] forms the basis of a paradigm called "weak textualism" (as a counterpart to the "strong textualism" of the postmodern philosophers).[163] The peculiarity of social entities lies in the fact that – contrary to what Ingarden may have thought – they are *real*, while at the same time being *dependent on the subjects*. However, what makes them exist is not an intentional act but an *in-scription*, i.e. the recording of an act[164] in some medium or other. This observation renders the assumption of the existence of a collective intentionality somewhat superfluous: the constitution of a social object depends on

160 We have borrowed this term from Francesca De Vecchi, "Ontologia sociale e intenzionalità: quattro tesi," *Rivista di estetica* 49, n. 1 (2012), 183–201.

161 Maurizio Ferraris, *Documentalità. Perché è necessario lasciar tracce* (Roma-Bari: Laterza, 2009).

162 See Ferraris, *Documentalità*, 140; Francesca De Vecchi, "'Platonismo sociale?' In difesa del realismo fenomenologico in ontologia sociale," *Rivista di estetica*, 50 n. 2 (2012), 75–90.

163 The concept of "strong textualism" can be summed up by a famous phrase by Jacques Derrida "There is nothing outside of the text [Il n'y a pas de hors-texte]" in *Of Grammatology*, 158. The change of perspective in weak textualism is based on the observation that a natural object does not need our conceptual frameworks in order to be real. See Ferraris, *Documentalità*, 34–38, 131–132, 360.

164 If, in a general sense, this term is synonymous with "action," the idea that we want to express here is that of an externalization or realization. In this sense, the act belongs to the external world, i.e. to the realm of expressions rather than of intentions.

establishing our intentions in acts capable of specifying its function. Indeed, no social entity – from credit cards to bus tickets, from universities to weddings – could exist without a registered act. In other words: "nothing *social* exists outside the text."[165]

This principle might be seen as too restrictive: there are indeed social groups, communities and even entire societies that do not have – or did not have for a long time – a written culture. We might reply to this objection by pointing out that what is too restrictive here is rather the meaning of what is meant by the "inscription" of an act. In order to account for such an inscription – and thus for the constitution of social entities – it is not necessary to use a text or writing in the strictest sense of the term (phonetic, alphabetic or notational writing); it suffices to refer to *any form of inscription and fixation of a trace*. We are thinking here of a more fundamental or archetypal form of writing, of what Jacques Derrida called "arche-writing [*archi-écriture*],"[166] a level that is superordered to the very distinction between orality and writing.[167]

To demonstrate how useful this argument is, let us take an act as common as a wedding. A wedding can certainly exist in a society without writing (in the strict sense); on the other hand, it could not exist without any form of memorization. The essential condition for it to be valid is not that it be notified in a register, but, in certain circumstances, that it be officiated in front of at least one witness deemed as being reliable. The pronunciation of two simple words ("I do") in the presence of a witness and in response to a specific question ("Do you, Josephine, take as your lawful spouse …") corresponds to what John Austin called a "performative utterance":[168] that is, in a few words, a speech act that is not limited to describing reality, but which gives rise to a new reality, i.e. the union of these two persons. Now, it will be said that their union is perfectly imaginable even without any witnesses; this is certainly so, but not this specific social pact that is a wedding. To exist, the latter requires the fixing of a trace: in this case, the trace might not be necessarily written down but, as we have just observed, it may be just entrusted to the memory of the witnesses (who will always be able to say: yes, that day they said "yes, I do" they both answered with those words to the person who asked them if they wanted to marry, and so they are married). Of course, such a fixation is generally less certain than that provided by a written document: the disappearance of any witness is likely

165 Ferraris, *Documentalità*, 132.

166 See Derrida, *Of Grammatology*, 56–60; Jacques Derrida, *Psyché, Inventions de l'autre*, t. 1 (Paris: Galilée, 1987), 86–87.

167 In this sense, the simple memorization of a rhythmic sequence by a student who hears his teacher clap his hands is an inscribed act.

168 John L. Austin, *How to Do Things with Words* (Oxford: Oxford University Press, 1962), 6.

to be problematic. The strength of such a commitment depends in any case on the persistence of a trace. What about a promise of marriage between two people who, a few seconds later, struck by a virus that temporarily erases short-term memory, forget everything they just said? The answer is that it does not commit them to anything – or, quite simply, that it does not exist, at least as a promise of marriage.

2.5 *Music as a Social Object*

At this point the reader might well ask what a wedding has to do with music. A lot, actually. And not just because weddings usually have music. Our idea is that from an ontological point of view, weddings and music must both be considered as social objects; and not only in a generic sense like the one we mentioned above, but in the sense that they both consist of an *inscription of acts*. I will now try to show how this is and to understand what constitutes music as a social object (in what way weddings and music are similar) and, in the following part, what characteristics make these entities more specifically musical works (and in what way weddings and music are not similar).

Like weddings, music is situated in space and time. This does not mean that it cannot be based on entities whose nature could be abstract or ideal (such as numbers or the principles of geometry); but it cannot consist, essentially or entirely, of such entities. At the same time, its existence depends to some extent on subjects (unlike natural objects, whose existence does not depend on them).[169] It should be emphasized once again that this dependence does not mean that such an existence can be perceived as subjective (nor, as Ingarden puts it, "purely intentional"). In the case at hand, these findings could be expressed as follows: to create music, it is not enough to imagine or emit any sound; that sound must be received by another subject who is willing to attribute musical meaning to it. If, before commencing the Kyrie of a Haydn Mass, a choir singer were to whisper something to their neighbour, a listener would probably not mistake these vocal utterances for musical sounds. The listener could, however, do so in another context: for example, by listening to the beginning of Luciano Berio's *Sequenza III* (the indication for the singer is "tense muttering"). Note that the latter example implies a principle of heterotropism: if Berio were the only one in the world to accept that such a vocal utterance could be considered musical, *Sequenza III* could not claim this title. However, a rather large (though not universal) audience, a certain number of

169 This argument implies the distinction between objects and subjects. In a very economical way, Ferraris, *Documentalità*, 8, invites us to define this difference from the notion of representation: for, unlike objects, subjects are capable of representation.

musicians, musicologists and listeners who practice this kind of music, not to mention institutions (festivals, concert halls, musical seasons, etc.), provide proof to the contrary: the "muttering" that Berio introduced into his composition is recognised in this context as a musical possibility in its own right (or can legitimately claim the status of a musical object). In other words, such muttering has (structural) characteristics that, in a given context (from a certain poetic, compositional model, etc.), allow it to function as a musical object.

It is important to note that a social object, while having a special ontological status, is not entirely detached, or detachable, from the natural world. Indeed, social reality is normally constructed "from" or "on" physical objects. An invoice exists insofar as there are subjects capable of recognizing it (as valid), but it also exists as a recording medium such as a sheet or a register. This does not mean, of course, that without paper it would not exist: as we have known for some time, a digital trace in a computer or a USB key (or an SD card, an external disk, a datacentre, etc.), is just as valid. Although much has been said recently about the digitization of documents, it should not be forgotten that even a digital trace in principle needs a physical medium in order to exist. What is important in any case is the possibility of producing and fixing an inscription: without this, there is no invoice.

Does this reasoning apply to the objects we are interested in? It certainly does and we should take a closer look at it. For there to be something like a song, a motif, a harmonic progression – in short, the whole vast galaxy of objects and forms to which we give the name "music" – there must be media capable of capturing a trace and thus making it possible to reproduce it. This fixation is fundamental at all levels: without it, a sound sequence would remain ephemeral and would not give rise to any musical object (or to the representation of any musical object, in the first case). Once again, as the ancients understood, Mnemosyne appears to us as the mother of the Muses. For what defines the musical object is indeed an inscription: a song remains the same song thanks to a trace that fixes its connotations. With the exception of a few details (which will be discussed in the third part), this point also applies when the trace is oral or recorded: in the first case, what counts is the exemplarity and repeatability of a performative act; in the second, the possibility of correctly decoding a signal encoded on the medium.

In short, any musical object can be explained as an inscription. This has to be related to the fact that its nature is fundamentally neither mental, nor ideal, nor moreover exclusively physical – even if the presence of a physical medium is indispensable to its existence – but rather, as we have just seen, social. We can consider as such music that is notated, but also musical performative acts, as well as musical recordings – which can, for their part, comprise the document of a performative act, or the realization of a creative act. Listening can also constitute an act, insofar as its result is a trace (such as a text, a drawing, or another kind of expression) that corresponds to a representation of a musical act. Here we enter, as Wittgenstein would say, into the language games that accompany musical practices and that structure aesthetic judgements in most cultures.[170]

But why should any musical object finally be conceived as an act? We are tempted to say that the main reason is epistemological: this category invites us to focus our attention on a form of *externalization* – in other words, on observable entities and events. In this way, we come closer to what Jean Molino and Jean-Jacques Nattiez call a "musical fact":[171] not a mental entity, nor a merely physical entity – such as a sound generated by the vibration of a body –, nor an abstract entity that would be mainly identifiable on a mathematical level, nor even an object merely linked to the functioning of our imagination, but rather a "social fact,"[172] that is to say an event that, while belonging to the outside world, is recognised on the basis of attitudes and categories that belong to a given culture. Now, the notion of a musical act corresponds precisely to this definition, while at the same time revealing more clearly – assuming that this is possible – the link that these facts maintain with the rules that govern social realities. Here is where the difference lies: while a fact – quite simply – *happens*, an act – in principle – *is produced*. In other words, it is the expression of one person addressing another. The awareness of this relational situation encourages a new look at the ways in which music is produced, interpreted and listened to.

To speak of musical acts (or acts in music) thus means to consider music from a perspective that takes into account an agent, intentions and a trace. It could be observed that the notion of act, even if it frequently refers to the idea of intention, is not necessarily related to it – indeed, it is possible to speak of involuntary acts. On the other hand, it is explicitly the idea of an intentional act that we turn to when considering the meaning of an act as a document. Now, this meaning may seem somewhat distant: when we think of a musical act, we are more likely to think of an action carried out by musicians than of a document. This impression does not necessarily put us on the wrong track. In fact, any musical object is very close to the status of a document. And it is

170 Ludwig Wittgenstein, *Lectures and Conversations on Aesthetics, Psychology and Religious Belief*, ed. Cyril Barrett (Berkeley and Los Angeles: University of California Press, 1967), 8–9.

171 See Jean-Jacques Nattiez, *Musicologie générale et sémiologie* (Paris: Christian Bourgois, 1987), 15. See also Nattiez, "Pluralité et diversité du savoir musical," 19.

172 See Molino, *Le singe musicien*, 76.

precisely in this sense that it refers to a relational context involving a trace, an agent and an intentional origin. A series of notes produced by a cat walking on a piano keyboard may be of musical interest in a more or less fortuitous way; but it cannot be considered as a musical act (and this despite the musicality that the animal may have displayed). The situation is obviously different if the sound sequence appears in a recording made by a person wishing to produce a result that can be appreciated by an audience, as in the *Catcerto* (2009) by the Lithuanian composer Mindaugas Piečaitis[173] – an example that brings us back to the necessary conditions of the presence of a trace and of a heterotropic intentionality.

2.6 *From the Document to the Work*

Musical works therefore are, as we have just seen, social objects – that is, basically, acts or documents. This is a necessary ontological condition. However, one could say that it is not yet sufficient: clearly there are documents that are not musical works. So what is the point?

To answer that, we first need to think about their function. Briefly put, a musical work is produced with the aim to affect or to move someone. In other words, it is usually conceived for arousing feelings in an audience. Exactly what kind of feelings and what audience is certainly open to debate; but an artwork which in principle aims to leave us indifferent seems to be a contradiction.[174] It is true that sometimes a document can have a similar strong emotive power: if the notification of an award is a source of joy, a parking fine can ruin anyone's day! Here, however, feelings 1) occur accidentally and not intentionally and 2) concern only the person rewarded or fined. As to 1): it can be assumed that those who awarded someone the prize (or the fine) do not only have the aim of arousing a certain feeling in them. On the other hand, in the case of artworks, it would seem contradictory to say that nobody had the intention of producing any effect at all on someone. As for 2): the feelings aroused by an artwork do not concern only one person: they are generally considered as disinterested and universal, valid (in principle) for everybody.

How can an artwork arouse such feelings? In looking for an answer, one can think, as we have already observed, of a certain symbolic functioning: a syntactic and semantic density is manifested in objects conceived to solicit an

173 See https://www.youtube.com/watch?v=zeoT66v4EHg, accessed on 19/09/2019. For information on Mindaugas Piečaitis: https://en.wikipedia.org/wiki/Mindaugas_Pie%C4%8Daitis.

174 As stressed by Maurizio Ferraris, *La fidanzata automatica* (Milano: Bombiani, 2007), 166–168.

aesthetic reaction that involves certain perceptual and cognitive skills.[175] Now, an entity conceived to function in this way is properly an "artefact," i.e. the product of a technique. Such an object must be distinguished, in its essential way of being, from natural entities.[176] As we have seen, it is appropriate to consider it in the light of social objects. But in a way, an artefact is *more* than just a social object. Indeed, while the essential properties of social objects depend "not on their material base but on revocable human intentions," the properties of the artefacts depending on revocable intentions seem not essential.[177] Take this example: if a government decides to cancel the 5€ note, this money would simply no longer be valid (it would no longer have the social properties that allow us to buy a sandwich with it). Now, a government might decide, for example, that Stravinsky's *Rite of Spring* will no longer be heard in concert or that it will be used as a simple stimulus for cows in order to produce better milk: it remains a fact that the *Rite of Spring* would continue to have the same aesthetic properties – the properties one could grasp when it would be correctly "activated."[178] The case seems similar to that of a screwdriver, which continues to exercise its function – that is, to screw or unscrew the screws – even if it is systematically used, say, as a toothbrush. In short, a *Rite of Spring* that is no longer heard in appropriate conditions would remain a musical work, even if in fact it no longer functions as a musical work.

Another point should be mentioned: if a musical work is an artefact, this implies that it *must* have an author to whom we can attribute the intention to shape such an entity. Of course, this does not mean that we must know who the author is and what are the particular intentions he had at the time he created the work (in this case very few people would listen to musical works!). Rather, we must be able to attribute (at least in principle) to the one who generated those sounds *the intention*, albeit very basic, *to produce music* (and not, say, a mere moan, a cry for help, an order, etc.). For example, we might not necessarily know who composed a traditional dance tune recorded in Val Resia (*de facto* very often the composer remains unknown in traditional music): what matters is that we have to be able to suppose that whoever invented this dance did it to produce music. But, again, take a monkey walking on the keys

175 As pointed out by Nelson Goodman, *Ways of Worldmaking* (Hassocks: The Harvester Press, 1978), 67–70.

176 This was observed in a famous passage of Aristotle, *Phys.* 192b.

177 See Marconi, Diego, "Artefatti e oggetti sociali," in *Ermeneutica, estetica, ontologia. A partire da Maurizio Ferraris*, ed. Tiziana Andina and Carola Barbero (Bologna: il Mulino, 2016), 213–223.

178 See Nelson Goodman, "L'art en action," *Les Cahiers du Musée National d'Art Moderne* 41 (1992), 7–13.

of a piano: is it able to generate a musical work? Precisely as in the case of the cat we mentioned earlier, I think we can say that, even if it *could* produce a pleasant or aesthetically interesting sequence of sounds, it would be difficult to answer affirmatively (can we really accept that a monkey could have the intention of producing such an object with such a specific function?).[179]

Here therefore is a definition that allows us to understand *when* there is a musical work (to put the argument in Goodman's terms): there is a musical work when we encounter *a sound artefact based on a trace having a normative value and designed to function aesthetically*. In other words, a sound artefact whose specific identity consists in its aesthetic functioning;[180] if we add the condition that this artefact has to deal with sounds and silences, we arrive at a concise definition of what a musical work is. It should also be noted that such an artefact may present itself in an autonomous form (as a "simple" sound artefact) but that it tends, in most cultures, to present itself in multiple forms of association with other media and forms of expression: with acts of speech (vocal music), choreography (popular dances, ballets, etc.), drama on stage (musical theatre), narration with moving images (cinema, video art), etc.

Can we now affirm that any sound artefact with an aesthetic functioning and which is based on a structure with normative value is in fact a musical work? The answer is "yes" in our opinion, but only on the condition that the (aesthetic) properties of such an artefact appear to us as artistic properties, i.e. characteristic of the social system of production and evaluation which, for us, in a given culture, is the art of music. To highlight the value of this condition, let us take an example. We may well find that the sound of the bells of the church of Saint Maurice in Strasbourg is particularly nostalgic or poetic and therefore attribute aesthetic properties to it. The reason why we might hesitate to accept this sound as a musical work is not based on the presence or not of these properties, or on a questioning of what appears, in every respect, as an artefact. It is rather that the context in which we ordinarily appreciate the sound of church bells does not generally imply the identification of an (explicit) artistic-musical intention. Could a change of context make us hear this sound sequence as a work? This is certainly not impossible. Many ancient and modern cultures for example do in fact practice the art of the carillon. One might say that the latter situation is quite different: these are performances

179 One might wonder if this question also applies to robots. Although I think that a robot cannot be said to have the intention to create a musical work, its products could be considered as musical works insofar as they are the indirect result of the intention of the person who programmed it with the intention of creating a musical work.

180 See Roger Pouivet, *Qu'est-ce qu'une œuvre d'art?* (Paris: Presses Universitaires de France, 2007), 66.

that correspond to a practice that is traditionally recognised as musical, and as such can take place within a system of appreciation – sometimes even a very refined one. If we take away the performance, there is nevertheless still the construction of the carillon, which can sometimes be particularly sophisticated – for example, to remain in the same context, that of the astronomical clock in Strasbourg Cathedral. We could consider this as a work produced in the light of a "watchmaker's art," even if it still might possibly have a musical interest.

So how do we know if we are in the presence of a musical work when we examine a performance or a practice in a given (cultural) setting? To answer this question, it is necessary to examine the contexts in which the artefact is produced and received. When this is problematic, we can begin by investigating various kinds of clues, such as the features of the object that reveal which type of production it belongs to; or the marks that accompany it and which reveal aspects that carry a certain value or that attest to the intention of the creator of the artefact to produce a musical result. Fundamentally, it is a question of realizing that what is, to a certain extent, considered as artistic is only recognised as such (i.e. perceived as art) according to a pre-existing way of perception or conception in the culture where the object was forged.[181] The attribution of such a qualifier depends on the tastes which, in each society and at each moment or period of its history, determine that an act has an artistic significance. Thus, it should be possible to "test" whether such an act is the subject of a judgment based on particular language games, whether it elicits a certain response from listeners, and whether it is part of a practice to which a certain artistic value is ascribed.

To sum up, a sound structure is a work when it reveals that it functions aesthetically and when we can identify an artistic-musical intention in it. Several aspects can be indicative of the presence of such an attribution of meaning, including the signs that accompany the artefact and that focus our attention on its origin (composer, context) or on its belonging to a known musical style or genre. But we should be careful not to misinterpret such a finding. Indeed,

181 We thus come closer to a criterion that Jerrold Levinson established as the basis of his historical and intentional definition of art (Levinson, *Music, Art, and Metaphysics*, 3–25). This definition is recursive and, as is well known, is subject to considerable problems; see Paolo D'Angelo, "La definizione dell'arte," in *Introduzione all'estetica analitica*, ed. Paolo D'Angelo (Roma-Bari: Laterza, 2008), 24–31. Nevertheless, we believe that the basic intuition that underpins it is a good one and may make sense for a researcher working in the field: the impossibility of providing a strict definition of what art is should not deter any attempt to identify, within a given cultural framework, a set of artefacts that a society tends to categorize as artistic.

these are not necessary and sufficient conditions, but rather symptoms whose shared presence teaches us that we are dealing with a work. One could formulate this rule in the negative: if, in a given case, it proves impossible for us to focus our attention on *any* of its aspects (i.e. on a pattern that enables us to identify the musical object in a given context; on an aesthetic functioning; on an artistic value and intention), it seems to us frankly inappropriate to speak of a musical work.

But again: how is the presence of such an artefact detectable in a given situation? The most basic answer would be the following: by locating an inscribed act associated with a sound structure within the framework of a practice recognised as musical.[182] It should be stressed that the idea of inscription and trace takes us beyond the physical dimension of the artefact; rather, as we have already pointed out, we are getting closer to what has been defined as an "indicated" and then "partly abstract" (sound) structure[183] and which could also be understood, according to Stephen Davies,[184] as an Aristotelian universal,[185] a "type" or a "kind" consisting of prescribed sound events. In other words, there could not be a work if the sequence we can read, perform or reproduce was not accompanied by a constraint that can be expressed in this banal way: "this is how the sequence must be presented and not in any other way" (with, in many cases, some important specifications: "this is how it must be performed, with such and such an instrument, or how it must be varied or embellished, in order to be properly instantiated, etc."). The object, here, is socially constructed and identified: in addition to being based on a kind of inscription, it is associated with artistic intent and shared forms of appreciation and shared standards. Normativity is expressed on several levels, but above all in the terms of a more or less formalized prescription and addressed to all those who wish to make the artefact work aesthetically.

It can be observed that, in the most ordinary situations, what allows us to confirm the presence of such normativity is generally a certain (state of)

182 Attempting to find out whether a practice is to be considered musical is not necessarily doomed to failure insofar as we are able to gather enough information in the context of production and reception. Thus, the cantillations of the Koran, while clearly having musical components, will not be considered in Persian culture as a performance or a musical work (see the discussion on this subject conducted by Jean-Jacques Nattiez, "Pluralité et diversité du savoir musical," 20); on the other hand, this could well be the case for a Balinese gamelan (which also has a ritual and religious function. We will pursue this example in the third part).

183 Levinson, *Musical Concerns*, 46.

184 Davies, *Themes*, 32.

185 In the sense that what is considered universal does not exist a priori, but only from the moment of its first realization in a concrete instance.

completion of the trace. The latter is visible and delineated, even if such delineation sometimes appears as imposed from outside, such as in the applause of the audience. Equally revealing is the presence of labels (inscriptions in codes or symbolic systems of different genres or nature) that are generally indicative of an auctorial intention or more generally of what, in a given context, stems from a willingness to participate in processes of artistic-musical creation.[186] The object's convergence or co-presence derives from its belonging to an artistic tradition and its status as a candidate for evaluation based on aesthetic criteria shared by a broad group of people.

This observation brings us fairly close to the institutional theories of art.[187] It does not, however, oblige us to accept the idea that we can rely on an "artworld"[188] defined by a main institutional framework. Today, this idea is in conflict with the considerable multiplicity of artistic and musical genres and practices. Indeed, it should be admitted that there are several evaluation criteria corresponding to the different contexts and forms of life in which works are appreciated, judged, explained and commented on (but also sometimes criticized, blamed, etc.). If we take a close look at the ways in which aesthetic judgements operate, we can see that the status of a work that has been effortlessly granted to a musical object in one context becomes less visible or even totally invisible in another. Now, to understand when this happens in a given relational framework, it is useful to identify some sign of the composer's intentions (even if presumed or coinciding with an anonymous group) or some mark of the object likely to meet a judgement criterion. If we then want to grasp the internal reasons that justify the assessment, we will have to examine the operation of shared criteria that are generally linked to particular language games.[189]

To sum up, a musical work is a *sound artefact based on a trace having a normative value and designed to function aesthetically*. In addition to being the result of the inscription of a perceptive reality – the perceived sound event/

186 Here one must take into account the innumerable terms likely to accompany the presentation of the work: titles, signatures, chronological or stylistic indicators; but one could also extend this notion to all kinds of *parerga* that frame the object (curtain, scene, etc.). See Pietro Kobau, "Parerga," *Rivista di Estetica* 40 n. 1 (2009), 21–39.

187 We are thinking in particular of the one proposed by George Dickie, *Art and Aesthetic: An Institutional Analysis*, (Ithaca – New York: Cornell University Press, 1974).

188 As is well known, this notion was introduced by Arthur Danto in the homonymous article – "The Artworld," *The Journal of Philosophy* 61 (19), 571–584 –, which however was limited to conceiving it in terms of a theoretical atmosphere, and not as an institution; see Andina, *What is Art?*, 38.

189 See Yves Michaud, *Critères esthétiques et jugement de goût* (Paris: Jacqueline Chambon, 1999).

object – in a system of musical references, such an artefact also calls for supplementary inscriptions (embellishments or *parerga*, external traces or paratexts) and forms of "subtle" appreciation, i.e. based on shared criteria in an artistic and relational context. What allows us to identify such an object are specific capacities referring to categories, evaluation criteria and language games shared by a community of creators/producers/receivers.

2.7 *From 4′33″ to 1000 Years* (*via 0′00″*)

Is there not a risk that the conception of the musical work that we have just outlined might be called into question by some of the musical productions of the avant-gardes of the last century? Let us take a famous example: in John Cage's *4′33″*, we do not hear a single note produced by the performer (usually a pianist, as per David Tudor's first performance, though Cage actually conceived it for any instrumentalist). In this work there are instead three intervals of silence of the (total) duration of 4 minutes and 33 seconds. How could a sound artefact based on a trace with normative value be identified here if there is no sound? Could it not be imagined that, more radically, anything – and thus also a moment of absence of sound – could become a musical work, provided that an artworld accepts such a premise?

Let us try to answer those objections. First of all, to be precise, Cage did not wish to set silence to music (an idea that in itself was not new[190]), but rather to draw attention to the environmental noises that inhabit it.[191] The desire to pay attention to these types of sounds, and more precisely to consider them as a new kind of music, stems from a pantheistic intuition inspired by oriental philosophies.[192] The experiment, like others dating from the same period, was intended to show that music, even before being a work, is something that happens, some kind of event.[193] Its message is that the composer should leave

190 We can mention the *Marche funèbre composée pour les funérailles d'un grand homme sourd* (1893), by Alphonse Allais (a score entirely made up of empty pentagrams, in line with the monochrome paintings by the same artist and accompanied by equally humorous titles: *Récolte de la tomate par des cardinaux apoplectiques au bord de la mer Rouge*, or *Première communion de jeunes filles chlorotiques par un temps de neige*), but also *In futurum* (1919), by Erwin Schulhoff, a piano work composed solely of pauses and silences. See Andrew Kania, *Silent Music*, "Journal of Aesthetics and Art Criticism" 68 n. 4 (2010), 343–353.

191 See Carmen Pardo Salgado, *Approche de John Cage. L'écoute oblique*, Trans. in French by Nathalie Lhuillier reviewed by Hélène Olivesi (Paris: L'Harmattan, 2007), 52–53.

192 See Davies, *Themes*, 15–16.

193 Considering these aspects, Davies, *Themes*, 26, concluded that 4′33″ is not a musical work but rather a "happening" or, more precisely, a "performance piece about music." The same piece has been conceived by Alessandro Bertinetto, "4 minuti e 33 secondi di arte. Non

the sounds as they are. However, 4′33″ comes in the form of a signed score published by an established music publisher (Edition Peters[194]): a title which, despite its minimalist character (one only reads the conventional mark "Tacet," three times), places the performance in a well-ordered framework. Within the specified time frame, the sounds must somehow be "authentic"; i.e. they must not appear as sounds that have been intentionally produced or organized by the musician. There would be no problem if the pianist coughed; more problematic, on the other hand, would be a situation where, while coughing, the performer inadvertently hits a key. How should we take such a note? Is it part of the ambient sounds, and therefore part of the work, or is it a mistake? Cage specialists will probably have an answer for us. But what should be noted above all is that intervals of silence are in fact intervals in which what is to be silenced is *music in the traditional sense*, i.e. sounds organized and structured on musical staves. 4′33″ is a conspiracy against this organization – and paradoxically a well-organized or regulated conspiracy, with precise durations for each of its movements: 30″, 2′23″, 1′40″.

But what is the meaning of these durations – and of the total duration of the work? Here are a few remarks about this. 4′33″ is neither too long nor too short: what we experience is unlikely to tire us (even if for some, it may already be too much!). At the same time, it is long enough to allow us to grasp all its nuances (to listen to the ambient sounds you need concentration!). It falls within what we could call the "window of opportunity" of an ordinary music listening experience (even though it is a little bit longer than what is today called a "hit"). In fact, these durations, in addition to implying a chronometric performance, conform perfectly to a criterion to which most objects that aspire to become works of art are subjected: that of "mesoscopy," i.e. the fact that a given object/event, if it wants to reach our senses, must be of "medium" size. In short, far from proving that everything can become music, 4′33″ seems to demonstrate that it is appropriate to focus on a *certain kind of entity or event*.

Against this conclusion it could be argued that such a duration is not absolutely necessary, since it has been randomly decided by the composer. Moreover, as far as one can speculate on its symbolic value (in seconds 4′33″ corresponds to 273, and -273° is the value of absolute zero on the Celsius scale), such a precise rule is not crucial from a musical point of view; would the situation have been really different if Cage had written "4 minutes and a half," or "about 4 minutes"?

---

di musica," in *John Cage. Una rivoluzione lunga cent'anni*, ed. Giacomo Fronzi (Milano: Mimesis, 2012) 172–174, as a work of "sound art."

194 These aspects have been duly highlighted by Nattiez, "Pluralité et diversité du savoir musical," 19–20.

It might as well be deleted. Cage fans will not be able to cry sacrilege, since the composer himself conceived what resembles version 2.0 of his piece: 0′00″ (1962).

Does such a work demonstrate that we can also bypass the principle of mesoscopy by widening (or narrowing) the horizons of the art of sound *ad libitum*? Nothing could be less certain. The work is based on a single instruction, or rather it comprises only one instruction: to stage a disciplined action and make it the object of maximum amplification. What is the point of this? Given the context of its production (the fabulous sixties, when Cage was already known for his musical philosophy), we can hazard a guess: in general, this piece confirms that in music, what is important is not what is truly "composed" but rather what is manifested by the performance event itself; it is as if it tells us: "the music is here, please, don't look for it elsewhere!" More precisely, the action is designed to focus our attention on the ambient sounds that mark its unfolding. Perhaps it is to invite us to penetrate this (generally elusive) background which explains why it is *isolated* and *amplified*: we must be able to listen to what we would normally exclude from the realm of music (sounds that have not been intentionally composed, free to express themselves in all their natural fragrance). But this means that what we hear is an event of a certain duration that is usually quite limited (you can see this by looking at the performances that have been filmed and posted on the Internet, starting with the one by Yoko Ono, the artist to whom Cage dedicated his work).[195]

On the other hand, it is true that there are some surprisingly short compositions. Many of us will be familiar with Anton Webern's concentrated miniatures (the second of the *Drei kleine Stücke* for cello and piano op. 11, from 1914, which lasts barely 25 seconds). But in pop or rock music we have an even better example: the song 'You Suffer' by the *Scum*, the first album of the grindcore band Napalm Death is in the record book, clocking in at only 1.316 seconds. It seems that the band played it in all their concerts. Watching the performances on YouTube, it is extremely difficult to hear, amid a searing scream, the four words that make up its text ("You suffer … but why?"). But after all, maybe the musicians couldn't have cared less about their intelligibility (if they did, they would probably have opted for a longer duration). The most crucial point in this barely prolonged moment is the explosive emergence of a sound that has all the characteristics of the metallic distortion of this musical genre.

What about the other end of the durational spectrum? While nobody (at least to my knowledge) has ever written a millisecond song, someone has on

195 The work was also dedicated to Toshi Ichiyanagi, a Japanese composer and student of Cage (in addition to being Yoko Ono's husband at the time).

the other hand sung a song for 52.4 hours non-stop[196] and someone else has even created a millennial work. The former example, as surprising as it may seem, does not pose a problem in theory: listening to a 52.4-hour song is certainly an endurance test, but it is still a possible experiment. The second example, on the contrary, seems to defy all limits, going far beyond the duration of a human life. How can this be remotely possible?

The work bears the eloquent title of *Longplayer*. It is generated by a computer that processes a sample of acoustic instruments.[197] Playback began at midnight on December 31, 1999.[198] You can listen to it on the Internet (http://longplayer.org) or go to one of its public listening places (one is in the Millennium Dome's relaxation area in London; others are in the United States, Australia and Egypt). According to the instructions given by the composer, British multi-instrumentalist Jem Finer, playback will continue without pause (and without rehearsals) until midnight on December 31, 2999, when the piece will be performed *da capo*.

All well and good, but what exactly does the person who clicks on this link listen to, or – if they prefer to try an original experience – go to one of the places mentioned above (perhaps making sure beforehand that the work is still running: in times of economic or health crisis, careless site owners might have decided to pull the plug)? What they hear then is background sound of metallic resonances comprising for the main part of Tibetan gongs and bells being struck and scraped in various ways. It sounds a bit like some "environmental" music created in the 1970s. The fact that we can adjust or freely manage the duration of our experience seems to echo an idea that has inspired many sound installations by contemporary artists.

Rather than invalidating the theory, this example allows us to better understand its scope. The fact that the installation is listed in the Guinness Book of Records confirms (if it were still necessary) its exceptional character. It can be understood precisely as a borderline case of what we normally do not consider as a musical work. Indeed, as no one can ever listen to it in its entirety, we

196 This is the American musician and film music composer Mark Mallman (the session, *Marahon Two*, was held in 2004 at the Turf Club in St. Paul, Minnesota).

197 More precisely, the work "results from the application of simple and precise rules to six short pieces of music. Six sections from these pieces – one from each – are playing simultaneously at all times. *Longplayer* chooses and combines these sections in such a way that no combination is repeated until exactly one thousand years has passed" (see this website: https://longplayer.org/about/how-does-longplayer-work/).

198 The end of the millennium has been at the origin of other experiments of this kind. One of the most famous is the performance of the organ version of the piece "As slow as possible," composed by John Cage in 1987, at St. Burchardi church in Halberstadt, Germany: started in 2001, it is scheduled to last 639 years, until 2640.

cannot state that *Longplayer* coincides with a re-identifiable sound structure. All we can re-identify here are (seemingly random) combinations of sounds emitted by a family of instruments (metallic idiophones). Using Goodman's arguments, one would only have to ask: how might we take, perform, copy or plagiarize such a work?

It should be noted that *Longplayer* is not a musical work intended for performance (even if it results from a performance); as it has been recorded and programmed it is intended instead for playback. It can therefore be assumed that with the right equipment (a computer with a digital matrix recognition algorithm) one could identify the exact combinations of the sound sequences that are played back. But no one could be sure that what is reproduced is really *this work*: we do not know if tomorrow, the day after tomorrow or in 70 years the sequence will change, making us understand that what we thought was a copy or a faithful reproduction was nothing more than a quotation, perhaps of a few hours, two months or even 70 years (what are these durations compared to a whole millennium?). All we can be certain of is that someone took or copied a small part or possibly the idea of the work, and thus created a similar installation with similar sounds.

What can we learn from this? Perhaps this: *Longplayer* is a sound installation that we can enjoy for as long as we like, but certainly not for a thousand years. Within a (much) more limited time, we listen to seemingly random combinations of recorded metallic resonances. We know that what we enjoy is part of an organized whole. Is this knowledge enough to make the object of this experience a millennial musical work? I would say the answer is no, or at least a dubious "neither yes nor no": with this knowledge, we can only assume that what we are dealing with is a kind of conceptual artwork, and that what we are listening to is the part of an object that we are assured we will never be able to appreciate. In short, of a musical work that can resonate "a thousand years in the world and a thousand more," the most we can say – as the Italian songwriter Fabrizio de André did in speaking of our human souls[199] – is that it presents itself as a "beautiful deception."

2.8 *Conclusions*

In this part we have examined the nature of musical works and defended the idea that they are social objects, and more specifically *sound artefacts based on a trace having a normative value and designed to function aesthetically*. This concept enables us to take into account their own objectivity. It should

199 Notably in the song "Anime salve," composed with Ivano Fossati and published in the album of the same name in 1996 by the Ricordi label.

be emphasized that this choice does not minimize the many contributions of the studies that have been conducted on the acoustic aspects or the cognitive and psychological strategies involved in the production and reception of such objects. On the other hand, it does allow us to remove the results obtained by these approaches from the risk they often run: that of leading to a form of physicalist or psycho-cognitive reductionism. Realizing that a musical work is fundamentally a social entity resulting from an inscribed act constitutes a basis for studying its different modes of aesthetic functioning, as well as how it presents itself in our experience. Indeed, as we have had the opportunity to observe, many works, recorded on disc do not have real-time performance; while some involve performance on a given instrument, others do not require it at all; still others explicitly prescribe variations that are realized in the performative act. If one wishes to propose an adequate explanation of this multiplicity, it will be necessary to examine the different artefacts in question, paying particular attention to the kind of normativity that characterizes them. This is what we will try to do in the next part.

3 Orality, Notation, Phonography

3.1 *A Typology of Musical Works*

Studies in musical ontology have focused mainly on musical works notated on a score, especially music from the Classical-Romantic period, jazz improvisations,[200] and more recently rock music.[201] In contrast, theoretical approaches have dealt less frequently with the world of orality or have attempted to compare different types of works as a whole. Among these approaches, the one developed by Stephen Davies is undoubtedly one of the most significant, since he formulated a typology capable of reflecting a broad segment of contemporary musical practice. We will therefore begin this part by considering the criterion on which such a perspective is based.

200 Starting from the essays by Alperson (1984) and Brown (1996) already mentioned in part 1.

201 While an "inaugural" thesis on rock music had already been formulated by Theodore Gracyk, *Rhythm and Noise: An Aesthetics of Rock* (Durham: Duke University Press, 1996), the debate underwent an important development especially after 2006–2008, with numerous articles published in the *Journal of Aesthetics and Art Criticism*, including Andrew Kania, "Making Tracks: The Ontology of Rock Music," *Journal of Aesthetics and Art Criticism* 64 (2006), 401–14, and other essays published in Europe, such as the books by Pouivet, *Philosophie du rock* and Frédéric Bisson, *La Pensée rock: essai d'ontologie phonographique* (Paris: Questions théoriques, 2016).

Davies invites us to consider the general class of musical works according to a fundamental distinction: on one hand, works for performance and on the other, works for playback. He also distinguishes between works intended for "live performance" and works intended for "studio performance."[202] We will examine the implications of the second distinction a little later, but first we need to focus on the superordinated distinction. Its interest is immediately apparent if we compare a Chopin *Étude* for piano and an *Étude* by Herbert Eimert: where the former requires a performance in order to fully exist, the latter does not need one at all. In this sense, an instance of Chopin's work produced automatically by a computer, using a software programme (such as "Finale" or "Sibelius") able to playback the score, could not be considered as valid, because such a work was explicitly designed to be performed; on the other hand, Eimert's work can only be presented by reproducing the recording of the original tape, for it was not conceived to be performed but reproduced (with a suitable device).

We therefore think of musical works as basically being performances involving a human agent or "mere" technical reproductions. It should be noted that this dual possibility, perfectly valid today, was not always so in the past. Indeed, that a musical work can exist without there being a performance – and that music can therefore free itself from the constraint of being a performative art, like dance or dramatic art[203] – has only been possible late in human history. When exactly? One would be immediately tempted to say from the moment recording was invented, at the end of the 19th century. But Davies points out that the possibility of reproducing music without the use of musicians already existed long before that time, in particular through the many devices designed to produce mechanical music: Pianola, chimes, etc.[204] Musical works which do not require an actual performance therefore have "a long historical pedigree."[205]

This remark is accurate: some of those devices enable a musical artefact to become autonomous (and have done so since the sixteenth century). We would be right however to assume that, with a few exceptions,[206] works for such devices were adaptations of pieces for which an actual performance was

202 Davies, *Musical Works and Performances*, 6.

203 As observed by Godlovitch, *Musical Performance*, 3.

204 Among the oldest devices, we can mention the "mechanical drum" or "war drum" designed by Leonardo da Vinci (see drawing in the *Codex Atlanticus*).

205 Davies, *Themes in the Philosophy of Music*, 36.

206 Such as Mozart's *Fantasia in F minor for mechanical organ* (1791), K 608. In the 20th century works were written for Pianola by composers such as Casella, Hindemith, and Stravinsky. See Pierre-Henry Frangne and Hervé Lacombe, "Introduction. Musique et enregistrement:

also (or could also be) envisaged. In other words, a set of chimes or a Pianola had to be presented as supplements able to reproduce, in a correct but inevitably reduced form, what could also have been played by live musicians. And if, at first, the early wax roll recordings seemed to give the same results, it soon became clear that audio recording had consequences of a very different sort. With this invention, the documenting of an actual human performance and the fixing of an original and autonomous sound construction became possible. The first result was achieved by the use of the phonograph (invented by Thomas Alva Edison in 1877) and the gramophone (introduced by Berliner in 1888 and intended for greater commercial success). Insofar as it "instigates the reproducibility, in principle infinite, of the same performance," it actually calls into question for the first time the idea that every musical performance corresponds to a "unique and irreversible experience."[207] The second result became possible in the mid-twentieth century, when the development of magnetic tape recording made it possible to create works that were entirely indebted to this new system of fixing/recording the trace.

The history of phonography has in fact been marked by several stages corresponding to technological progress. Among the most important, at least initially, was the electric recording,[208] a transition that coincided with a remarkable improvement in sound quality that gave the listener access to a relatively faithful sound image of the original source. In an article written in the 1920s, the writer Paul Valéry expressed his enthusiasm for devices that made it possible to "reproduce a musical work at will" and to do so "anywhere in the world, at any time."[209] Valéry was an exceptional witness to an upheaval that characterized the ways of experiencing music: at that time, music had become somewhat autonomous, because it was subject only to the will of the listener, without involving the (contemporaneous) action of the musicians. In the 1950s, the editing work enabled by multitrack technology opened up new horizons for the world of music, and little by little a new paradigm of musical creation came into being. Instead of creating a score to govern a performance,

---

rupture ou continuité de l'art musical?," in *Musique et enregistrement* ed. Pierre-Henry Frangne and Hervé Lacombe (Rennes: PUR, 2014), 15.

207 Frangne and Lacombe, "Introduction. Musique et enregistrement: rupture ou continuité de l'art musical?," 19.

208 See Tournes, *Musique! Du phonographe au MP3* (Paris: Autrement, 2011), 44–52; Jacques Hains, "Du Ruleau de cire au disque compact," in *Musiques. Une encyclopédie pour le XXIe siècle. 1. Musiques du XXe siècle*, ed. Jean-Jacques Nattiez (Arles and Paris: Actes Sud and Cité de la musique, 2003), 911–915.

209 Paul Valéry, "La conquête de l'ubiquité," in *Œuvres. Tome II: Pièces sur l'art* (Paris: Gallimard, 1960), 1284–85.

musicians began to focus on recording their own performances in the studio. With the help of a producer and a sound engineer (roles that were destined to become increasingly important) the musicians were now able to choose, filter, mix and manipulate what they recorded until they obtained the desired result: a recording intended to be used as a master for the production of a multiplicity of discs that would contain the exact reproduction of their creation.

It was not the first time in the history of music that such a radical transformation in how traces were fixed had taken place: a few centuries earlier, in the Middle Ages, a musical world still largely dominated by orality had gradually been transformed by the development of so-called "mensural" notation. With this, entirely new pieces, with a much more complex and articulated structure, were born. A first "technological revolution in music"[210] was thus achieved, with changes in the ways the trace was fixed playing a determining role both in the morphology of the works and in their normativity, as we will see in more detail later in this part.

Since musical works could not exist without a system of recording to ensure their existence in historical time, we will establish their typology via the identification of their primary mode of trace fixation. This aspect seems to be more fundamental from an ontological point of view than the (still crucial) question of the relationship to performance underlined by Davies' approach (to which for other aspects we will remain generally close). The way in which works are created, their morphology and the aesthetic properties they are supposed to possess depend to a large extent on the way in which their trace is conceived and fixed. It is on the basis of this observation that we will consider, with François Delalande, the three "technological paradigms"[211] or ways of organizing musical cultures: orality, notation and phonography.[212] In the first, the trace is constituted by a mnemonic pattern or outline embodied in a model act that governs the creation of a musical object that can be adapted to multiple situations. In an oral context therefore, there is a framework in which important divergences can occur between the model and its concrete realization. When the trace is fixed by means of a notational system, these

210 François Delalande, *Le son des musiques. Entre technologie et esthétique* (Paris: INA-Buchet/Chastel, 2001), 32.

211 François Delalande, "Le paradigme électroacoustique," in *Musiques: une encyclopédie pour le XXI*^e^ *siècle. Vol. 1 Musiques du XX*^e^ *siècle*, ed. Jean-Jacques Nattiez (Arles and Paris: Actes Sud and Cité de la musique, 2003), 541–543.

212 With slightly different terminology, this tripartition has been highlighted by several scholars; see for example Simon Frith, "L'industrialisation de la musique et le problème de la valeur," in *Musiques: une encyclopédie pour le XXI*^e^ *siècle. Vol. 1 Musiques du XX*^e^ *siècle*, ed. Jean-Jacques Nattiez (Arles and Paris: Actes Sud and Cité de la musique, 2003), 1140.

divergences tend to diminish. Finally, when it is recorded, the work is returned to us through decoding and sound reproduction, which effectively eliminates the need for the performative act.

Historical time →

Oral work		
	Notated work	
		Phonographic work

As we have already said, this tripartition corresponds to a historical progression: over time, we have gone from an era when the fixation and transmission of music was done orally, to an era marked by the spread of notation (from medieval polyphony to contemporary music) and then to our present times where we have turned to the use of recorded media (from electronic music to rock and pop). We emphasize that these three options are not mutually exclusive: orality continue to exist even in musical cultures mainly based on notational systems; in cultures based on recording, some kinds of notation (and of orality) continue to play their role. According to Davies,[213] important differences can be highlighted in the identification of a more or less "thick" structure: orally transmitted works, being ontologically "thin," lend themselves more easily to adaptations and arrangements; the variable part in works based on a score is reduced somewhat and tends to be even more reduced until reaching "zero level" in phonographic works, which have been considered by some scholars as ontologically "saturated."[214] We can outline several main differences:

Recording	**Medium**	**Culture**
Memorisation	Neurons	Oral
Notation	Score	Written
Audio recording/encoding	Disc, digital file	Phonographic

213 Davies, *Musical Works and Performances*, 10–11.

214 Roger Pouivet, *Philosophie du rock. Une ontologie des artefacts et des enregistrements* (Paris: Presses Universitaires de France, 2010), 63. As we will see a little later on (see §3.5), the transition to digital environments seems to partly disprove the assumption of a complete ontological saturation of phonographic works.

The multiplicity of carriers is linked to the differences in the way the "systems" function and, ultimately, to the organization of a musical culture. The passage from one recording system to another has been accompanied, in fact, by an increase in the level of normativity of the sound structures that identify the work. In orality, the trace is sometimes – depending on each local tradition – only a simple canvas for variations which are in turn delegated to musical practice. Take a divinatory song of the *Fataleka* tradition (in the Solomon Islands): it will be identified as *the same song* even if it is produced with some variations in timbre or rhythm (on condition that an essential pattern is not undermined). In contrast, a Beethoven sonata cannot be presented by changing some notes, even if a pianist still has a lot of freedom to create a certain sound, or a certain phrasing, etc. We are even more restricted with a work of electroacoustic music (ontologically "thick"): we cannot present it by changing some sounds, or by filtering, cutting or modifying some of its frequencies (in this case it would be a new work which has been derived from the previous version).

Let us now take a closer look at what characterizes these three types of works, their contexts of production and reception, their aesthetic functioning, and their effective implementation.

3.2 *Oral Works*

For the reasons that we have already discussed in the first part, the concept of "oral work" is perhaps the one most likely to cause problems among philosophers and musicologists alike. Let us begin by mentioning some objections to it.

a) The concept is (far) too generic to be used in "field research." To conduct such research, specific terms from the cultures examined should be used: the Inuit *katajjaq*, the *trazzu* from the Sardinian tradition, the *raga* from the Indian tradition (or should classify the musical practice based on the instruments used, such as the *gbofe*[215] from the Tagbana community,[216] etc.).
b) It is, at the same time, too particular and too connotational, because it designates phenomena situated in a very specific historical and cultural framework: that of Western art music between 1800 and today (which could possibly be extended to neighbouring practices, but without going too far, at the risk of appearing horribly ethnocentric).

---

215 This term refers to a transverse trumpet and, by extension, the songs and dances it accompanies.

216 Approximately 180,000 individuals living in northeastern Côte d'Ivoire.

c) It insufficiently reflects the specifically processual dimension of musical orality.
d) It is ambiguous, because the term is etymologically linked to vocality – whereas it is normally also used to indicate many instrumental musical practices.

a) To the first objection, we can reply that even in a comparative discourse the use of a generic term is sometimes useful. As we have seen in the first part, the question is not whether a culture possesses the term "musical work," but rather to see whether, in its characteristic practices, we can identify sound structures with normative value and a kind of appreciation that may allow us to adopt this concept. This does not contradict the (very appropriate) use of more specific terms according to the context.

In other respects, the idea of comprehending something such as an oral work may seem debatable: we could argue that it is just another manifestation of Western ethnocentrism, which is always inclined to find its own hallmarks in the culture of others. It should be recognized, however, that it is very difficult for a culture today to ignore the functioning of works that has imposed itself with globalization. History shows that no civilization has ever remained completely impervious: we must therefore neither ignore the role played by the interests of large multinationals, nor reduce everything to a problem of imperialism or economic colonialism. For the sake of better order in these concepts it would be more appropriate to keep our eyes fixed on the fact that local cultures no longer seem (except in rare cases) to be able to remain outside of any exchange, outside of a global network. This network has spread ideas and behaviours everywhere that were once geographically circumscribed and has promoted contacts and cross-fertilization between them – and not always in a negative way.[217] Ethnocentrism would be more like "limiting" the existence of works of music to our own culture based on notation and writing.

b) Let us take a lullaby sung by a Pygmy Aka woman (in the Republic of the Congo) appearing in a video clip posted on the Internet by the Congolese ethnologist Sorel Eta.[218] This is a piece with a clear function: as in most cultures, it is assumed that it is sung at bedtime (although this is by no means a certainty and in this particular case the result is far from certain!). In any case, there are some features that could lead us away from the notion of work. A transcription of what is heard will have no normative value. One need only

217 We share on this point the optimism of Jean Molino, *Le singe musicien: essais de sémiologie et d'anthropologie de la musique*, ed. Jean-Jacques Nattiez in collaboration with Jonathan Goldman (Arles: Actes Sud/INA, 2009), 201–202.
218 YouTube: http://www.youtube.com/watch?v=u4Fepb3bE98.

listen to other performances of this lullaby to become aware of this:[219] we are listening to only one of the possible variants (rhythmic, melodic, polyphonic) of what at first glance is only a common pattern: the "exploration" of an octave in ostinato, produced with a vocal utterance (which, to an European ear, is reminiscent of the *yodel*) found in other vocal expressions of this people.[220] Nor do we know whether what we have just heard shows a "signature" or a more individual mark. The singer will not claim to have "created" this lullaby; but she could claim to have sung it correctly. It is doubtful that she can name the author of the song; she will probably say that one of her relatives taught it to her. It should also be noted that the identification of such a musical object is based on the identification of a conventional title ("lullaby"); it would then be useful to check whether this label (with its function) was applied to it by the researchers who examined it (by virtue of its resemblance to other phenomena) or whether it corresponds to an original designation. Anyhow, taking such a performance out of its context and placing it in an institutional or recreational context – such as a concert hall – would be tantamount to distorting it, making it play a role that the Pygmy Aka would never have intended.

Why do we hesitate to use the notion of work here? The crucial issue is not really the *function* of the song, but rather the *structural role* that this culture attributes to the pattern or model implemented and/or to the performative act. The singer adapts or varies a model that we can clearly recognize in her rendition: a musical unit endowed with a symbolic function. Are we so far from the notion of work (as we have defined it)? Or should we say that this music is mainly improvised?

We should turn to some specialists who can give us some answers. Simha Arom has observed that this musical culture has a precise classification of repertoires, genres, pieces, and to designate these, this culture uses terms that denote "both the social function of the musical event, the type of dance attached to it and the percussive pattern – obviously linked to dance – common to all the pieces belonging to this category and performed for this function."[221] As

219 See *Berceuse Aka*, a documentary made by François Gaulier and Alain Epelboin, CNRS Audiovisuel, Meudon, 1988 (http://www.youtube.com/watch?v=5yEikm4wKiY). The action takes place in the heart of a banana plantation near the Akungu river. The baby is cradled by his father, according to the role he plays among the Aka people (in other clips posted on YouTube); however, we see women accompanying the song by clapping their hands: (http://www.youtube.com/watch?v=E-EfWMv16iA).

220 In the anthology of songs edited by Simha Arom, *Centrafrique: anthologie de la musique des pygmées Aka* (Paris and Arles: Radio-France and Harmonia Mundi, 2002), 2 CD with a booklet, this vocal utterance is notably found in pieces labelled as "divination songs."

221 See the booklet of the mentioned CD, 4.

for the performative act, it is constantly subordinated to precise metric, rhythmic and melodic parameters.[222] Now, in our case, the woman observes a set of patterns (rhythmic or melodic sequences) as well as a certain way of singing. All of these recognizable elements constitute the outline which allows the listeners to recognize and hear the song *as an Aka lullaby* and not, for example, as a Mbuti wedding song. In these pieces, a performance is in effect still categorized as a rendering. It is a particular kind of rendering, in which the identity of the object resides in its outline which, in most cases, requires the performer to reproduce it with *adaptations* and *variations*. "Even though they do not engage in abstract speculation about their music," Arom observes, "the Aka are well aware of the theoretical elements of their music and the rules of their application: one need only look at the reaction to a mistake made by one of them to be convinced of this."[223] If an error is detected this would imply that there is a reference (more or less implicit) to a pattern (rhythmic or structural) that allows the listener to identify the object in question – which is in principle less clear-cut in improvised music (i.e. whose initial pattern seems in itself insignificant and whose interest lies *mainly* in the variations produced by the musician). All these aspects call for the use (prudent, certainly, but nevertheless certain) of the notion of work. To a certain extent, we can affirm that this woman's activity implies the intention to perform a musical work of the Aka culture.

As we have observed in part 1, the transmission of pre-existing musical units to the performative act (which are identifiable in their essential connotations by the members of a group who are responsible for their transmission) can be considered a common feature of most musical cultures of the world. An example borrowed from a very different context can provide us with eloquent proof of this. In Balinese gamelan music, observes Stephen Davies, a virtuoso piece like *Teruna Jaya* (played all over the island) is clearly recognizable even though "each group introduces its own modifications and variations and, over the years, continues to alter its account of the work."[224] Perhaps, adds Davies, it was already to some extent the way in which Roman, Ambrosian or Coptic song had been passed on.[225]

c) The temptation to oppose process and object is strong here.[226] However, on closer inspection, we have no interest in underlining such an opposition.

---

222 *Idem.*
223 *Idem.*
224 Davies, *Musical Works and Performances*, 22.
225 Davies, *Musical Works and Performances*, 22.
226 Patricia Carpenter, "The Musical Object," *Current Musicology* 5 (1967), 56–87, looked at this opposition to define what differentiates Western and non-Western cultures.

Let us note first of all that, even if the processual character of oral musical heritages is clearer than in score-based repertoires, it is not absent in them. The fact that a composer has "fixed" his intentions in a score does not ensure the total immutability of his work in historical time: performance styles change, and the same goes for our ways of listening, as has often been pointed out. Let us note, on the other hand, that what we hear, when we listen to a song similar to the one we have cited, *is a certain result, not the process as such*: we are dealing with an *act* – that is, *a process that has been carried out*, or that has been "actualised." Moreover, if this song, as it appears to our eyes and ears, takes place in a temporal process, it is also true that it is characterised in our experience and in our memory of it by a certain stability over time: we can compare it to other, more or less similar results, and grasp its morphology.

This observation should not lead us to suppose that everything can become a work or, even worse, that the notion of work can exhaust everything we can find in the vast field of musical orality. Let us stress once again that this field contains many instances that better convey the idea of exercising a performative activity responding to a different normativity from that which governs the performance of works. For example, it can be said that a poetic-musical exercise such as the jousting sung in "*ottava rima*" by the "*poeti a braccio*" in central Italy[227] is clearly more an act of improvisation, since one of the most important aesthetic properties on which the public's attention is focused is the singer-poet's ability to invent on the spot (and not to reproduce a given structure).

d) This remark is in our opinion correct, because what musicologists focus on above all, when they speak of "orality," is not so much the vocal or verbal nature of a piece (contrary to what the etymology of the word "oral" actually means, which is derived from the Latin *os, oris*, the mouth), but on how the music is made and transmitted.[228] But despite the approximation – or perhaps by virtue of the existence of a more precise label, that of "vocal music" – the term has indeed become habitual. We now have two possibilities: 1) to replace it with an expression that is better able to account for the phenomena studied; 2) to accept it as a metaphor whose value is heuristic. As we do not have other conventional terms that are more functional, this second option would seem to be preferable. However, even if we use the term "oral" to refer to a certain way

227 See Cristina Ghirardini, "La 'naturale acuta sensibilità all'armonia, al numero ed al metro.' L'improvvisazione poetica in ottava rima in Italia centrale dal Settecento alla prima metà del Novecento," *Fonti musicali italiane* 22 (2017), 55–89.

228 Let us recall here, with Molino, "Qu'est-ce que l'oralité musicale," 487, that the notion of "orality" was originally introduced by linguistic and literary studies, notably by Walter Ong, *Orality and Literacy: the Technologizing of the World* (London New York, Methuen, 1982).

of transmitting music, it is not appropriate to set it apart from everything that is "written." Rather, we should point out the differences in the way in which the more general phenomenon of inscribing a trace (without which there would be no culture, oral or written) applies to such different means of fixation as the memory of a group of listeners or a score.

Let us then say that, like any musical work, an oral musical work is presented, from our perspective, as a social object resulting from a recorded act; what differentiates it from other artefacts of the same nature (i.e. social) and which makes it a *work* in the proper sense is its aesthetic functioning and its belonging to a system of artistic production/reception; what makes it an *oral* work is the fact that the trace is established – often anonymously – in the memory of the musicians/listeners and its transmission is done by means of example. It is therefore normal that, in this kind of artefact, creation, performance, improvisation and variation end up being grafted onto each other. In other words, the implicit rules of its enactment provide for a wide range of variations, adaptations and arrangements of the trace – which here has value as a model.[229]

Like any musical work, an oral musical work results from the inscription of a perceived entity – a sound structure – that operates within a framework of references that are recognised as musical by a group of at least two people.[230] In other words, it is necessary for a performative act to go beyond its purely transient or event-driven nature in order to manifest a trace. Someone might then observe that such a perspective is inappropriate to the situation under discussion: if there is one area in which the trace and the document are missing, it is definitely orality! Once again we reply that, from the point of view of this essay, the ideas of trace and inscription transcend the difference between the oral and the written. Let us return to the example of the Pygmies: although these people do not have any kind of notation, they *do* have, as we have seen, regulated vocal and instrumental practices. The production of polyrhythms as complex as those found in the records published by Arom that we have mentioned requires great precision on the part of each musician. All of them clearly follow a rhythmic pattern that has been inculcated in them due to prior training: it is a kind of "engram" or internal writing – since a behavioural pattern has been established and consolidated in the memory of the members of

229 See Simha Arom, "Réalisations, variations, modèles dans les musiques traditionnelles centrafricaines," in *L'improvisation dans les musiques de tradition orale*, ed. Bernard Lortat Jacob (Paris: Selaf, 1987), 119. See also Jean Molino, "Qu'est-ce que l'oralité musicale?," in *Musiques: une encyclopédie pour le XXIe siècle. Vol. 3: Musiques et cultures*, ed. Jean-Jacques Nattiez (Arles and Paris: Actes Sud and Cité de la musique, 2005), 491.

230 See above §2.5.

this group. This memory – or set of memories – is in principle the one and only medium that ensures the existence of these works (which means that these works would eventually disappear as members of such a community died off).

Saying that the transmission of these works is done by means of example means that it involves an act of imitation, which is never a simple copy that entirely conforms to the original. As Jean Molino observed when applying the concept of linguistic and literary phenomena to music, one of the features that best defines the world of orality is probably the "impulse for variation."[231] More generally, we will say that what is produced within the framework of an oral musical culture oscillates between the two poles that we highlighted in the first part: the "art of the trace" and the "performative art."

Such an oscillation can easily be detected. We have already mentioned the Sardinian *canto a tenores* tradition. In the vocal practices of this island, such as the *trazzu*, the performances are the results of a particular singing technique and the variation of several rhythmic, harmonic or melodic modules, which in principle do not constitute actual pieces. However, the ways of performing and transmitting this singing vary according to the place. In a study devoted to the vocal tradition of Castelsardo, a village in the province of Sassari, in the northern part of the island, Antonio Lai observes: "Neither chance nor improvisation can intervene in the creation of traditional pieces. One of the most remarkable aspects of Castelsardo's vocal specialisation is the extraordinary ability of the *cantori* to reproduce, even years apart, the exact same proportions between formal sections within the works in the absence of the temporal landmarks typical of the score-based musical tradition."[232] It can therefore be said that this town has its own repertoire of traditional songs, whose survival is ensured by a community that functions according to its own rules: there is a selection of voices, competitions between singers, "informed listening," and

---

231 "What folklore specialists in the 19th century and ethnomusicologists in the 20th century highlighted," Molino notes, "is the existence of different versions of the 'same' music: you never hear exactly the same folk song, the same oral epic, the same work from a traditional repertoire twice. This variation extends to the units of the musical system: it is the very margin of variation of each 'note' that often bothered the first ethnomusicologists and led to the use of analytical methods inspired by phonology. We are so accustomed to the rationalization of the musical system that we believe that a note can only be defined by the exact value of a frequency: before the rationalization of musical systems, their units functioned exactly as the units of linguistic systems still do, i.e. by using all the margins of variation allowed by the configuration of each system." Molino, "Qu'est-ce que l'oralité musicale?," 488.

232 Antonio Lai, *Recherche et création entre tradition écrite et tradition orale: pour une nouvelle musique sarde*, Mémoire d'Habilitation à diriger les recherches (Université de Paris 8, 2011), 45.

"demanding criticism both inside and outside the brotherhood."[233] The aesthetic functioning is clarified through the identification of a group of people who can be considered experts in the production of this type of song. This could amply justify recourse to the notion of a work: perfectly identifiable sound structures pass from one generation to the next and survive over time with their own artistic value.

Let us take another case that we mentioned above, the Inuit *katajjaq*. In this singing practice, certain modes of vocal articulation generate rhythmic sequences in which one voice appears both complementary and antagonistic to the other. Can we argue that two Inuit women engaged in this type of performance are performing a "work" of their culture?

In our view, this statement can be valid only in a very broad sense; in a more precise sense, it seems incorrect, as it would imply an excessive extension of the concept. Indeed, the rhythmic patterns and the type of phonation that we hear do correspond to a way of singing common to the expressions of this musical genre more than to a sound structure implemented in the performance itself. Nevertheless, the performance itself is subject to a value judgment that takes into account the ability of the singers to respond immediately to each other's rhythmic and vocal demands. Even if the *katajjaq* is in principle a game, and in particular a "throat game,"[234] a competition with a winner and a loser, victory is apparently not the main thing: it is rather a question of having fun, of enjoying a peaceful social interaction.[235] Once again, it should be left to the specialists to decide whether this is a *musical* game. On the other hand, it is appropriate to recognize that such a game, in the end, is more about the idea of a performance art than an art of the trace. One could say the same about a performance of Mongolian *khöömii*. The lighter or more provisional the model on which the musicians base themselves, the more difficult it will be to identify the presence of a work. Conversely, if the structure of the object we are examining is sufficiently developed and stable, we will not hesitate to use this category. This could, for example, be the case of a Friulian "villotta": a piece whose structure is perfectly recognizable in its basic shape, often accompanied by a whole series of revealing labels: title, town or geographical context of provenance, and period. But, once again, this does not mean that any musical

233 Lai, *Recherche et création entre tradition écrite et tradition orale*, 45.

234 See Jean-Jacques Nattiez, "Pluralité et diversité du savoir musical," in *Musiques. Une encyclopédie pour le XXIe siècle. 2 Les savoirs musicaux*, ed. Jean-Jacques Nattiez (Arles/Paris, Actes Sud/Cité de la musique, 2004), 21–22.

235 Nicole Beaudry, "Musique et jeu: l'exemple des autochtones d'Amérique du Nord," *Musiques et cultures. Une encyclopédie pour le XXIe siècle. vol. 3*, ed. Jean-Jacques Nattiez (Arles/Paris: Actes sud/Cité de la musique, 2005), 705–706.

object of this culture should be "forced" into this category. We should only use it within a boundary that we will have to keep up to date, paying attention to the appearance of new forms of trace inscription and the different ways of organizing musical practices.

We should be just as careful with certain expressions specific to musical traditions shared between writing and orality. To describe the function of the *radif*, which is essential to understand the art of commentary and paraphrase specific to the "literate" musical cultures of the Near East, Jean During remarks:

> By identifying the implicit rules, the overall aesthetics, the main lines of these melodies, the performer gradually discovers their organizing principles from which he can create other composed or improvised forms. Indeed, the *radif* is more than a "work" because it constitutes an aesthetic and technical standard, but less than a "work" because its destiny is to undergo transformations, to be recreated at each performance with a variable rate of unpredictability.[236]

The study of oral transmission in other musical cultures will make us encounter situations just as intermediate and nuanced as this one. This leads us to recognize that if the difference between the art of the trace and the art of performance, just as that between work and performance, must be clear in conceptual terms, in the study of concrete reality we have no interest in treating it as a binary antinomy: the "logical space" between these two poles is, so to speak, a space gradually populated by examples likely to attest to their proximity to one or the other. Thus, it should be noted that in musical cultures based on traditions of oral transmission, improvisation as such is never totally free; it is more easily found in two forms that Molino has proposed to call "improvisation-variation" and "improvisation-composition."[237] In the first case, the performances are conceived (and perceived) as "variants of a pre-established model that serves to identify the piece being played"; in the second, there is "a performance whose outcome is recognised as an original work: the criterion that allows us the distinction is a criterion of identity." The music produced by the peoples of Central Africa (as in the quoted example) fall into the first category; that of North India, Arabia, Iran or Turkey fall into the second. Now, in the second case, performance looks like a "creative" improvisation, in which the outcome "is not the realization of a model, or else the word is given an altogether different meaning entirely: it is based on a modal

236 Jean During, *Musiques d'Iran: la tradition en question* (Paris, Geuthner, 2010), 252.

237 Molino, "Qu'est-ce que l'oralité musicale?," 505.

system – such as a *raga*, *maqam* or *radif* – which functions as a framework for the composition." For this genre of performance, Molino proposes to adopt the formula of "compositions in real time" and to consider them as works; but as it is necessary to postulate an instantaneous creation, we nevertheless prefer to continue calling them improvisations, emphasizing the dual role played here by the performance.[238]

In summary, we can say that in an oral musical culture the performance of a work usually contains a form of adaptation and variation. Performing a popular song by exactly imitating what has already been done by others is certainly always possible; but the outcome will normally be considered insufficient, or even bad, or else as the exception that proves the rule. A more common and aesthetically functional approach will be to perform it with variations that refer in their turn to a repertoire of gestures, behaviours and attitudes, etc., regarded as conventional within a musical culture. Consequently, in analysing the performance of an orally-transmitted work, it would be pointless to apply the principle of *Werktreue*: rather, we would attempt to identify the underlying models, to identify a typology of variations, and examine the forms of adapting a given harmonic, rhythmic and melodic pattern.

3.3 *The Notated Work and Its Interpretation*

In my view, a notated musical work is a work whose *main* criterion for the construction and fixing of its trace is an act of writing. I stress this adjective to point out that any work whose constitution is based on a kind of notation should not necessarily be considered as a notated work. The relevance of this remark is as much ontological as morphological. For example, musicians composing a work in a studio could use notation for jotting down harmonic grids, rhythmic sequences, riffs or melodic ideas (this normally happens in several musical genres): nevertheless, none of these traces could allow us to "sum up" the identity of the work that results (as we shall see better later) from the act of recording. Moreover, if we look at the historical development of musical notation from Greco-Roman antiquity to the medieval world, we realize that notation was not originally involved in the composition of musical pieces: it was only employed to transcribe them and facilitate the work of the musicians who were supposed to ensure their transmission orally; (it is not by chance that the oldest medieval notation appears as a schematic indication of the

238 Beyond the frontiers established by genres such as "traditional music" or "world music," we can find this creative model in live performances by an electro musician such as Mika Vainio, for example, or by a DJ. It seems on the other hand that we can talk more openly about oral works in the first case that Molino described.

cantor's gestures). If one examines some music from the fourteenth century, one will soon realize that the situation has changed: a simple procedure such as the retrogradation of a melody (i.e. reading it from the end to the beginning) is "unimaginable without the help of a graphic medium"[239] and shows, in fact, that writing profoundly influences the morphology of the work – which then clearly presents itself as a notated work.

As we have already observed, this type of work implies a different, more defined normativity than an oral work. However, the class of works that functions in this way includes, as with oral works, a wide variety of cases. The trace can be limited to indicating an essential gesture or morphology, as in ancient neumatic plainsong; it can indicate the relative or absolute pitch of sounds, as well as their duration, as in mensural notation; it can also indicate the way in which they are produced by means of an action exerted on an instrument, as in tablatures.[240] It is the adoption of a "notational system," which ensures the principle of "disjointness of the characters,"[241] that has allowed music to become what Goodman calls an "allographic art" – that is, as I have already mentioned, an art in which the criterion for identifying works is orthographic – and thus to confer on its traces a clearly higher degree of normativity. However, the progress that has led to the development of such a system is not linear, nor is it apparently a one-way street, as Goodman himself pointed out in producing some examples of graphic scores developed by the musicians of the avant-garde of the last century. Rather than proving that sometimes, in the history of the arts, "revolution is retrogression,"[242] I see this fact as a demonstration that, as we have already pointed out, trace-fixing systems are not mutually exclusive, but clearly pile up one on top of the other. At the same time, however, it is true that at a certain point one system ended up taking precedence over the others: most of what a Western musician played or produced a century and a half ago falls into the category of notated or score-based works; on the other hand, it would not be wrong to say that the works that most musicians of today produce are phonographic – without this making the composition of works based on score, nor, for that matter, the transmission of oral works, disappear.

---

239 Delalande, *Le son des musiques. Entre technologie et esthétique*, 33.

240 Stephen Davies, "Notations," in *The Routledge Companion to Philosophy and Music*, ed. Theodore Gracyk and Andrew Kania (London and New York: Routledge, 2011), 70–79, effectively summarizes these possibilities and illustrates many other details.

241 Nelson Goodman, *Languages of Art. An Approach to a Theory of Symbols* (Indianapolis: The Bobbs-Merrill Company, 1968), 133.

242 Goodman, *Languages of Art*, 190.

It should be remembered that, when a musical work is based on a notational system, this normally includes the indication of pitches and ratios of sound durations, while many other signs remain non-notational: for example, the tempo, the articulation and dynamics (indicated by signs such as "pp," ">," "sfz," etc.). However, in our view this does not mean, as Goodman suggested, that such non-notational elements make no contribution to the identity of the work: as Levinson has rightly stressed, the sound structure of a musical work surely also includes a certain tempo, "even when broadly specified."[243] In order to show this, it is enough to consider the fact that a work played at a tempo that differs radically from the one indicated by the composer (or from the one that can be regarded as suitable for a certain sound structure in a given context) will be difficult to recognize,[244] and this is probably true to a large extent also when the articulation or dynamics are radically changed: could the performance of a Beethoven symphony played entirely in pizzicato or staccato be considered a real token of the Beethoven symphony?

The question of tempo – as for the "wrong note"[245] – is one of the most discussed aspects of Goodman's view.[246] To avoid any paradox, it is better to openly admit that the identity of score-based musical works – whatever their form of notation – requires that their actual implementation is also taken into consideration: it is therefore necessary not to focus solely (from a contextualist perspective as Levinson proposed) on the instrument for which such works were conceived and on their production context; it must also be admitted that such works may be affected by a certain approximation and in no way be forced to respect the flawless identity provided by a purely notational system. In other words, common sense seems to us sufficient to recognize that "three wrong notes are not enough to disfigure the performance of a symphony containing tens of thousands of notes, and that ten thousand would disfigure it."[247] Putting this idea back to front, so to speak, we would like to suggest that the lack of precision in the marks of dynamics or tempo do not constitute a major defect but, on the contrary, represent one of the main issues of their

243 Levinson, *Music, Art, and Metaphysics*, 88.

244 For example, a listener with a basic musical background usually has some difficulty perceiving Offenbach's famous "Can-can" melody in the fifth piece of Camille Saint-Saëns' Carnival of the Animals ("Tortues"), even though this is clearly quoted.

245 "Since complete compliance with the score is the only requirement for a genuine instance of a work, the most miserable performance without actual mistakes does count as such an instance, while the most brilliant performance with a single wrong note does not." (Goodman, *Languages of art*, 186).

246 See Predelli, Stefano, "Goodman and the Wrong Note Paradox," *British Journal of Aesthetics* 39 (1999), 364–75.

247 Bernard Sève, *L'instrument de musique. Une étude philosophique* (Paris: Seuil, 2013), 301.

aesthetic functioning. For it is the very need to fill these gaps – and possibly to do it expressively – that has laid the foundation, in performance practice, for a true *interpretation* of the work (otherwise the latter would be useless: *in claris non fit interpretatio*), i.e. a performance based on free choice and a high level of mastery in the performative art, to best accomplish what the score only indicates partially. Beyond the fact that, as we just mentioned, the notation is generally deficient regarding all the possible nuances in a musical gesture, it should be mentioned that sometimes the work itself "partially escapes its composer," who cannot grasp all the possibilities of enacting a given composition.[248]

The idea of interpretation is to some extent consubstantial with the idea of a score-based work: it brings out its normativity, insofar as it seems to confirm "the transcendence of the work or of the text itself, through its infinite interpretability and the inexhaustibility of its meanings."[249] After all, it is precisely because an interpretation, in this class of performances, is recognised as a sort of necessary supplement that in an analysis – as we have already mentioned – we devote more attention to the deliberate deviations introduced by the musician in relation to the indications of the score. These deviations are what have often been considered, since Carl Seashore's inaugural work,[250] as crucial for explaining the "expressivity" of a performative act.[251] If conformity to the notation is an unavoidable rule, equally important, for the performance to be considered successful, is the ability to bring out the aesthetic properties which, in a musical culture, can be regarded as constitutive of the work (even without being explicitly pointed out by the composer). As any good musician knows, there are various ways of playing a staccato, a pizzicato, a *rallentando*, a slur and many other indications of this kind. So, more than being an instance of a work, the score could be understood, as Nicholas Cook has suggested,[252] as a sort of script: a set of instructions that has to be adapted to the situation, the sensitivity, and body of the player. However, despite its variability, it is indeed the performance, and not the score, which embodies a version of the work inclusive of all its aesthetic properties. Among the aims of analysing the performance of a notated work are: firstly, the identification of those

248 Anne Roubet, "Interprétation," in *Eléments d'esthétique musicale. Notions, formes et styles en musique*, ed. Christian Accaoui (Arles/Paris, Actes Sud/Cité de la musique, 2011), 260.

249 Mario Brunello and Gustavo Zagrebelsky, *Interpretare. Dialogo tra un musicista e un giurista* (Bologna: Il Mulino, 2016), 11.

250 Carl E. Seashore, *Psychology of Music* (New York: Dover, 1938).

251 Eric Clarke, "Understanding the psychology of performance," in *Musical Performance. A Guide to Understanding* ed. John Rink (Cambridge: Cambridge University Press, 2002), 63–66, shows how problematic such an assertion can be.

252 Cook, *Beyond the Score*, 260.

aspects that make it a successful interpretation (but also that make it conventional, original, exceptional, and typical, etc.). At the same time, it must be stressed that the aesthetic qualities of a performance of a notated work can *never be regarded as mainly autonomous*: compliance with the score's indications remains unavoidable (it may be more or less strict, but never absent). Other aims may also guide the analysis of a performance: for instance, showing how an interpretation reveals a form of understanding (or of "segmentation") of the work by the musician, or identifying the way in which the meanings and expressivity of the work are brought out.

In the 19th century, the development and diffusion of musical works was accompanied by an increasingly clear division of roles between composers and performers, as well as by the progressive affirmation of the *Werktreue* principle in which the musician undertakes to respect the composer's score, to make it his own while remaining faithful to his marks and intentions. Beyond the principle of orthographic conformity, there is also the question of bringing out the expressiveness that is specific to a musical style or to the performance practices of a given period. This idea seems normal to us today, but, as Nikolaus Harnoncourt rightly pointed out, it is far from being a general rule: in almost all periods of the past, the principle was rather one of arranging and adapting what composers had delivered to the present situation.[253] With the advent of the movement advocating the idea of a "historically informed" performance, the discourse changes and the musician undertakes to render the work as close as possible to what is assumed to be an execution of the period in question.

This normative implementation concerning score-based works was the subject of much discussion from the 1960s onwards. For a good twenty years, the principle that the music of the past should be performed as it was originally performed was at the heart of a kind of counter-culture that strongly influenced not only musicological debate, but also the musical world and the record market that was always closely linked to it.[254] The 1980s were nevertheless the time when many researchers seriously began to question the validity of such a project. Without going into the details of this debate – which would be well

253 Nikolaus Harnoncourt, *Baroque Music Today: Music as Speech. Ways to a New Understanding of Music*, transl. Mary O'Neill (Portland: Amadeus Press, 1982), 15.

254 See Nicholas Cook, *Music: A Very Short Introduction* (Oxford: OUP, 2000), 94–99 and Saama Sulaiman Marion-Gallois, "Le rôle du disque dans la promotion et la pérennité d'un paradigme interprétatif," in *Quand l'enregistrement change la musique*, ed. Alessandro Arbo and Pierre-Emmanuel Lephay, (Paris: Hermann, 2017), 69–90.

beyond the scope of this essay – we will, with Jean-Jacques Nattiez,[255] limit ourselves to recall the main issues raised by the idea of performing a work in the way it could have been heard when it was composed: these include doubts about the instrumentation and the number of musicians, but also the opportunity to adopt a more or less uniform playing style (such as *notes inégales*) or the opportunity to curb the expression of emotions (to the point of sometimes "neutralizing" them) in the performative act, not to mention the impossibility of integrating the network of meanings linked to the original context of the work into an interpretation.

All these difficulties have prompted scholars to question the judgement of this so-called "authenticity." In his book entirely devoted to this theme, Peter Kivy drew attention to what he proposed to call the "paradox of authentic listening,"[256] and concluded that the search for conformity to the original work should be rejected in favour of another idea of authenticity: one that requires the interpreter to be true to himself in his own interpretative choices. However, such a relativistic position can be confusing. Without renouncing the sincerity of the interpreter, there is no reason to doubt the morphological, structural or expressive characteristics of the work which are to be found in the score.[257] Take, for example, a version of Mozart's "Allegro maestoso" from the Piano Sonata K. 310 in A minor such as the one recorded by Glenn Gould:[258] it could be considered authentic insofar as it is faithful to a personal performative project,[259] in the speed and nervous, almost electrifying energy that runs through it from beginning to end; but, at the same time, it could not be considered valid, since the aesthetic properties of this Sonata are clearly not so nervous or electric and, moreover, an excessive speed risks erasing all the

---

255 See Jean-Jacques Nattiez, "Interprétation et authenticité," in *Musiques. Une encyclopédie pour le XXIe siècle. 2 Les savoirs musicaux*, ed. Jean Jacques Nattiez (Arles/Paris: Actes Sud/Cité de la Musique, 2004), 1133–1142.

256 This paradox lies in the fact that "the historically authentic performance movement, which is meant to restore to us historically authentic musical sound, does so only at the cost of destroying historically authentic sound: it gives us sonic authenticity with one hand and takes away, in the form of ahistorical listening, sensible authenticity with the other." Peter Kivy, *Authenticities: Philosophical Reflections on Musical Performance* (Ithaca: Cornell University Press, 1995), 70–71.

257 More precisely, drawing on an observation made by Margaret Bent, Nattiez proposes to identify what he calls the "local truths" of the work; see Nattiez, "Interprétation et authenticité," 1128–1148.

258 In Glenn Gould, *Mozart: Piano Sonatas Nos. 8, 10, 12 & 13*, Sony Classical (1972 Sony Music Entertainment).

259 This is what Kivy has called "personal authenticity": to be authentic "in the sense of authentically one's own, emanating from one's own person – authentic, in other words, as opposed to derivative or imitative." Kivy, *Authenticities*, 108.

differences in phrasing and themes. One might conclude that it is not ultimately a version of Mozart's work, but rather a kind of "work of performance"[260] by Gould that refers to Mozart's sonata in an important but ultimately insufficient way.

The crucial issue, after all, is to discern what the aesthetic properties of this sonata are – and thus what properties must be present in one of its performances in order to be considered a correct token of the work. To the extent that, as the analytical debate has often pointed out, there is no entity without identity,[261] the question is central for the ontological investigation of musical works and, as such, has informed the debate on the antagonistic perspectives of sonicism, contextualism and instrumentalism.[262] The debate between Kivy and Levinson mentioned in the second part constitutes a significant sample of this discussion. As we have seen, for Kivy it is a question of addressing the essential sound structure of the work, whereas for Levinson it is necessary not only to consider the structure "indicated" by the composer (at a given time and place), but also to consider it, even more specifically, as "inclusive of means of performance."[263] This option is also summed up by the idea of a "structure of performed sounds, as opposed to 'pure' sounds."[264] Thus, to show that an automatic reproduction in a computer-programmed version of the "Hammerklavier" sonata does not constitute a correct token of Beethoven's work, it suffices to know that such a reproduction would from the outset remove one of the aesthetic properties that contribute to its identity,[265] that is to say, its performative virtuosity. Nor would this sonata be the same sonata in a version for accordion or guitar, even if played with remarkable virtuosity because it was clearly intended to be played on a piano. Rather, it would be the (virtuoso) performance of a transcription or adaptation of the work – that is, to a certain extent, the performance of a new musical work, distinct from the original one, to which it obviously remains highly indebted. Finally a musical work based on a score must be conceived as *a sound structure rich in contextual properties and properties linked to its concrete implementation* (such as the pianistic character of a Chopin *Nocturne* or the violinistic character of a Vivaldi *Sonata*). It may be said that this richness probably already characterizes some oral works – whose properties must also be examined in the light of

260 On this notion see above, 29, and below, 85.
261 Willard Van Orman Quine, *Ontological Relativity and Other Essays* (New York: Columbia University Press, 1969), 23.
262 See Matheson and Caplan, "Ontology," 41.
263 Levinson, *Music, Art, and Metaphysics*, 78.
264 Levinson, *Music, Art, and Metaphysics*, 79.
265 Levinson, *Music, Art, and Metaphysics*, 76 and 240.

the historical, geographical and artistic context of its production, and certainly also in relation to a specific vocal or instrumental designation (an Armenian oral work will more easily retain its identity when played on a duduk than on an oboe). However, as we have seen, in the world of orality the margin of adaptation or adaptability of the sound structure is generally greater and the instrumentation is almost never explicitly prescribed and can therefore be considered as non-normative.

If score-based musical works are generally richer in properties, such richness can vary considerably from case to case. On the one hand, it is undeniable that the identity of several works composed during the Romantic period normally implies a "structure of means of performance": Chopin's Mazurka in A minor op. 17 n. 4, which Levinson chose to exemplify his idea of artistic indication,[266] will probably lose much of its salient properties if played on an organ (or, rather, it will have very different properties, since it will undergo important changes in timbre, sound balance and dynamics). But, to limit the scope of this observation, it must be pointed out that many musical works whose transmission has mainly been assigned to notation do not obey this rule (or at least do not obey it so strictly). As is the case for the *Art of Fugue*, many works of the Baroque era left a certain margin of freedom in the instrumentation: we need only think of the many sonatas intended alternately for oboe, flute or violin, or of many keyboard compositions which, at the same time, do not include the indication of a specific instrument (would the *Well-Tempered Clavier* played on a piano be one of the possible instances of the work or an adaptation?), not to mention the different possibilities for the realization of the continuo. We will say that these are relatively old examples. That said, a quick glance at certain contemporary compositions would show that the idea of a freer or more open instrumentation has far from disappeared.

Actually, the attitude of composers is variable: it has changed a lot over the years and continues to change today. Therefore, even though specific instrumentation is likely to play a major role in preserving the identity of certain notated works, this principle cannot be generalized. We might very well consider an arrangement as being the same work but this would certainly no longer be the case if we changed a great number of notes. A more "tempered" conclusion is needed: if the identity of score-based works includes a set of properties that is overall broader than those embodied in oral works, the quantity and the role of these properties is not deducible *a priori* but must be determined from contextual considerations relating to the production and reception of the artefact. In some ways this could rehabilitate what has been defended as

266 Levinson, *Musical Concerns*, 48–50.

historically informed performance: it is precisely via thorough knowledge of the contexts that we identify properties that can be considered as incidental or, conversely, essential to the work in question. Reversing the terms of the question, it can be said that producing historically informed performances remains a plausible task, despite the difficulties that such an attempt may entail.[267]

Let us look for a moment at the issue of score-based works that are recorded. Given that such works are intended (and expected) to be played by the composer as well as by the performers and listeners, the recording is in fact about a performance. It should not be confused with the act of performance itself, of which it constitutes a mere document.[268] In principle, therefore, such a recording requires a kind of transparency: it must be to some extent *true*.[269]

Nevertheless, the meaning and the implications of such "transparency" can be discussed. The term could make us believe that a recording is above all supposed to restore the acoustic or physical and phenomenal elements of its source. However, despite appearances, this assumption is fundamentally false. As is known, a simple change in the position of the microphones and in the quality and type of microphone used (e.g. unidirectional, omnidirectional, dynamic, condenser, etc.) can significantly change the sound image. The difference between the listening conditions of the source (a concert hall, auditorium, plaza, etc.) and the listening conditions where we actually listen to the recording (on a hi-fi system at home, with headphones or earphones, in the car, etc.) must also be taken into account: to create the acoustics of the Carnegie Hall – as observed by Eisenberg[270] – we would need to add some reverberation to the original sound recording (made in this concert hall), and to balance the frequencies and volumes, etc. This forces us to admit that, even if it must be possible to establish a direct link between a recording and its source, the former, far from being a sort of "duplicate" of the original sound, is rather a kind of "natural sample":[271] i.e., a copy having certain properties that also belong to what it refers to.

267 See Jerrold Levinson, "In Defense of Authenticity: Adjust Your Ears, Not the Music," in *Of Essence and Context. Between Music and Philosophy*, ed. Ruta Staneviciute, Nick Zangwill and Rima Povilioniene (New York: Springer, 2019), 185–195.

268 See Gérard Genette, *L'Œuvre de l'art (1): immanence et transcendance* (Paris: Seuil, 1994), 77; Godlovitch, *Musical Performance*, 14.

269 See Arbo, "Qu'est-ce qu'un enregistrement musical(ement) véridique?," 187–191.

270 Eisenberg, *The Recording Angel*, 90.

271 See Sandrine Darsel, "Musique et enregistrement. Une exploration goodmanienne des musiques du monde," in *Ontologie musicale: perspectives et débats*, ed. Alessandro Arbo and Marcello Ruta (Paris: Hermann, 2014), 194.

This principle obviously applies equally to notated and oral works. There may, however, be some distinctive features in the recording of score-based works that are worth pointing out. Consider a recording of a Beethoven sonata played by Sviatoslav Richter[272] and broadcast on Prague radio in 1959, and Glenn Gould's recording of Sibelius' piano works.[273] By their acts, neither Richter nor Gould *constituted* the work in the strict sense of the word; they merely *performed* it. However, whereas the first example concerns a single performance – and therefore a single sound recording – the second is more peculiar: the performer, through the mixing of several "takes," finalizes a token in which a change in sound levels is perceptible. Whereas in Richter's recording we feel as if we are in the middle of a concert hall, when we listen to Gould the sound source seems to move towards or away from us, as if in an "acoustic zoom" effect.[274] The recording appears as an artefact that does not hide the distance that separates it from a genuine "live" listening experience.[275] We would suggest calling it a "work of performance," insofar as it fixes a specific version of the work and renders it lasting. In other words, it constitutes an interpretation of the work and not a simple document of the same.[276]

A recording of a score-based work can therefore be seen both as the document of an actual performance – that is, one played at a given moment by a performer, which in turn constitutes a token of the type/work – and as the finalization of an interpretation of the work obtained through the selection, manipulation (and possibly editing) of the sound sequences played by the performer. The difference is not always as clear-cut as in the Richter and Gould examples mentioned above, and it may in fact escape us: even if there is something that points to elements of post-production (such as changes in the sound

272 *Sviatoslav Richer in Prague. Beethoven Richter*, 4CD, CDM/Harmonia Mundi (1993/1997), CMX 354022.25.

273 *Trois Sonatines* op. 67 et *Trois Pièces lyriques* op. 41 (recorded in 1976 and 1977): *Glenn Gould plays Sibelius*, Sony BMG, BOOOUH8HTY.

274 François Delalande (*Le son des musiques*, 19) considers "presence" as one of the important parameters of the sound in Gould's recordings: "The acoustic presence – near/far – but also a psychological, symbolic presence – intimate or distant, warmth versus coldness."

275 We are close to what Pierre-Emmanuel Lephay called a "recording-object." See "De l''enregistrement-témoignage' à l''enregistrement-objet' et vice-versa" in *Quand l'enregistrement change la musique*, ed. Alessandro Arbo and Pierre-Emmanuel Lephay, (Paris: Hermann, 2017), 43–44.

276 See Alessandro Arbo, "Qu'est-ce qu'un enregistrement musical(ement) véridique?," 182–183. The history of the disc over the course of the 20th and 21st centuries seems to have confirmed this possibility; as has been observed by Pierre-Henry Frangne and Hervé Lacombe, "Introduction," in *Musique et enregistrement*, ed. Frangne and Lacombe, 16, "the recording tends to constitute the interpretation as a 'text'."

balance, dynamics, spatiality or depth), this is generally not perceptible. This is hardly surprising, since one of the main tasks of a sound engineer is precisely to hide or conceal any imbalances, fixes or splices: the job is all about making us believe that an actual performance is taking place. The norm for recording notated music can be expressed as follows: to construct "what can be listened to as representing the reproduction of a singular performance from a privileged listening position"[277] (for orchestral music, this usually coincides with where the conductor stands at the podium). If Gould's recording does not coincide with such an idea, it is precisely because it is original in its attempt to enforce a way of listening that is emphatically different to what we expect in a concert hall.

But if the difference between the two cases mentioned is generally not detectable to the ear – in other words, if it is categorical and not phenomenal – why should it be taken into account? One reason is this: it is one thing to listen to an interpretation knowing that it bears the personal stamp of the artist – i.e. a product which, beyond the manipulations, mixing or simply rehearsal (one thinks of the studio recordings produced by Walter Legge[278]), is presented with all its qualities as a finished interpretation, capable of being reproduced an unlimited number of times –; it is another to listen knowing that it is a sound recording to which the musician has not had the opportunity or the possibility to replay, or knowing that it is a performance that took place at a given moment, in a given place, in principle in front of an audience (even if this audience were far away, as in the case of a radio broadcast). The two recordings differ in their aesthetic and ontological meaning. Despite appearances, they identify the particularities of the style of execution differently: it is what a musician intended to achieve in interpreting the work, or what he achieved in a more or less contingent manner in a single occurrence. It is to this categorical difference that one can relate the desire that pianist Claudio Arrau once expressed in an interview (which was mentioned, significantly, by Gould[279]): he was against the release of live recordings because, in his view, all the "stratagems" that the pianist might have adopted to satisfy a certain audience might appear counterproductive if they were to be heard again on a record.

In recordings containing "performance works," techniques of sound engineering or manipulation may conflict with the demand for truthfulness or

277 James Barrett, "Producing Performance" in *Recorded Music. Performance, Culture and Technology*, ed. Amanda Bayley (Cambridge: Cambridge University Press, 2010), 96.

278 See Eisenberg, *The recording Angel*, 95–98.

279 Glenn Gould, "The Prospects of Recording," in *The Glenn Gould Reader*, ed. Tim Page (New York: Alfred A. Knopf, 1989), 337–338.

transparency in document recordings. In the history of sound recording there is a famous episode involving the soprano Kirsten Flagstad:[280] she was not in top form during a recording session of *Tristan und Isolde*, and was replaced, at a specific point, by the soprano Elisabeth Schwarzkopf. The record producers concealed this fact but it nevertheless came to the ears of the public and critics and caused a scandal. Why the scandal? The answer has to do with the ambivalence mentioned above: even if this kind of record is the result of teamwork and can resemble, as Eisenberg pointed out, a film production (where the recording of a concert seems to have its counterpart in filming a stage play),[281] it seems normal, in the ordinary contexts of reception of a score-based work, to demand a kind of transparency from it (if Flagstad's name appears on the LP cover, it is indeed her voice and not someone else's that we expect to hear when purchasing and later listening to the record).

Gould's recording philosophy, like Herbert von Karajan's and, even more so, John Culshaw's, is an emblematic expression of what a work of performance is: the studio becomes a veritable laboratory where the performer's work continues.[282] If, in a general sense, post-production techniques are normally considered as being external to the performative act, it must be acknowledged that they sometimes turn out to be "musical gestures,"[283] as they contribute to perfecting the product of an interpretation (or better: where interpretation is seen as a product in itself, in a transformation that has sometimes been described as a form of "reification"[284]).

3.4 *The Phonographic Work*

In a broad sense, a phonographic work is a recording or, more precisely, an audiogram fixed on a medium. However, as we have just seen, not all recorded music is necessarily a phonographic work. So what does the latter comprise exactly? To answer the question, we need to go back to the main functions that a musical recording has, namely: documentary and constructive. If for

---

280 The anecdote is reported by John Culshaw, *Putting the Record Straight. The Autobiography of John Culshaw* (New York: Viking, 1982), 125.

281 Eisenberg, *The Recording Angel*, 92.

282 See Pierre-Emmanuel Lephay, "La prise de son et le mixage, éléments de l'interprétation: les exemples de Herbert von Karajan et de Glenn Gould," in *Musique et enregistrement*, ed. Frangne and Lacombe, 113–122.

283 Jacques Hains, "Du rouleau de cire au disque compact," in *Musiques: une encyclopédie pour le XXIe siècle. 1. Musiques du XXe siècle*, ed. Nattiez, 934–935.

284 See Peter Johnson, "Illusion and Aura in the Classical Audio Recording," in *Recorded Music*, ed. Bayley, 42.

the first,[285] recording means making the document of a singular musical performance reproducible – which, in turn, can constitute, as we have seen, the instance of a work or an improvisation – for the second, recording actually means engineering a work or, as we have just seen, one of its possible interpretations. It is precisely to this second option that we must refer when we speak of a phonographic work.

It is difficult to say exactly when the idea of phonographically constructing a musical object first appeared. At any rate, one of the first occurrences was in the 1940s, with the first experiments in jazz re-recording (attributed to the American saxophonist Sidney Bechet[286]) and Pierre Schaeffer's *Club d'Essai* experiments in Paris (1946–1963), and then especially from the 1950s onwards, when advances in multi-track audio recording technology (such as the famous 8-track device produced by the Ampex Corporation and used by the guitarist Les Paul, who christened it the "Octopus") made overdubbing operations possible. In *musique concrète* and in electronic music, subsequently subsumed under the broader category of electroacoustic music, the recording is no longer the mere document of the performance of a work – given that it does not pre-exist the recording – but *constitutes* the work itself.[287] It is precisely within this context of an "art of fixed sounds"[288] that a musical work becomes phonographic. Works of this kind may be the subject of public presentations (an

285 It is certainly already first from a historical point of view: from the perspective of the pioneers of phonography, "recording" meant generating a trace corresponding to a sound event and making it possible to duplicate and reproduce it acoustically. The latter function may already seem implicit in the former, but the one does not in fact imply the other: twenty years before Charles Cros proposed his project to build the "paléophone" and Thomas Edison patented the phonograph, in the "Principes de phonoautographe," deposited at the Academy of Sciences in 1857, Léon Scott de Martinville had described a system of synchronized sound stenography that made it possible to trace and read pronounced sounds, but not to listen to them again; see Elizabeth Giuliani, "Comment l'enregistrement s'effaça devant la musique," in *Musique et enregistrement*, ed. Frangne and Lacombe, 78–79 and Ludivic Tournès, *Musique! Du phonographe au MP3* (Paris, Autrement, 2011), 14–17.

286 It was then Miles Davies, in the 50's and 60's, who used the studio editing possibilities; see Laurent Cugny, *Analyser le jazz. Analyse du jazz, analyse de l'œuvre* (Paris: Outre Mesure, 2009), 59–60.

287 As Roger Pouivet, pointed out, it is indeed the ontological model of *constitution* – to be distinguished from that of *emanation* – that allows us to account for the way of being of this type of work; see Roger Pouivet, "La triple ontologie des deux sortes d'enregistrements musicaux," in *Musique et enregistrement*, ed. Frangne and Lacombe, 159–172.

288 Gilles Cabanes, "Le rôle de l'enregistrement dans la musique concrète," in *Musique et enregistrement*, ed. Frangne and Lacombe, 209–210.

implementation that can be distinguished from its mere "reproduction"[289]); however, by definition, they do not require an actual performance.[290]

A phonographic work is therefore not only morphologically but also ontologically different to a score-based (and an oral) work, since its constitution depends on a mode of conception and fixing of the trace of sound that is specific to it and is new. In fact, a phonographic work is highly dependent on technological progress. As Walter Benjamin said in the 1930s,[291] the technological reproduction of images and sounds, as it emerged in the twentieth century, is not a mere external phenomenon that accompanies the history of art, but a factor that can profoundly condition its nature. This shows, among other things, the importance of thinking about musical ontology – just like ontology of art and, more generally, social ontology – in a historical perspective. Jean Molino has rightly pointed this out: "technology and science are changing the furnishings of the world and the way of being of human artefacts."[292]

The category of phonographic works includes not only electroacoustic music, but, according to many scholars,[293] rock albums, and more generally all musical production where the primary work is the "sonic image"[294] encoded in

289 See Eric Maestri, "Si può interpretare la musica elettroacustica?," *Aisthesis* 6 (Special issue: *Ontologie musicali*, edited by Alessandro Arbo and Alessandro Bertinetto) (2013), 173–193.

290 Of course, this does not apply to *live* electronic music, a genre which explicitly enhances the performative moment and which consequently makes the conservation of the works particularly complex; see Simon Emmerson, "In what form can 'live electronic music' live on?," *Organised Sound*, 11(3), 209–219. See also Delalande's distinction (*Le son des musiques*, 35) between "instrumental electroacoustic music" ("in which the electroacoustic or computer apparatus is an extension or partner of the instrument or voice") and "electroacoustic music on magnetic tape."

291 Walter Benjamin, *The Work of Art in the Age of Its Technological Reproducibility and Other Writings on Media*, ed. Michael W. Jennings, Brigid Doherty & Thomas Y. Levin, trans. Edmund Jephcott, Rodney Livingstone, Howard Eiland & others (Cambridge, Mass. & London: Harvard University Press, 2008).

292 Molino, *Le singe musicien*, 387.

293 See Theodore Gracyk, *Rhythm and Noise: An Aesthetics of Rock* (Durham: Duke University Press, 1996); Andrew Kania, "Making Tracks: The Ontology of Rock Music," *The Journal of Aesthetics and Art Criticism* 64, n. 4 (2006), 401–414; Roger Pouivet, *Philosophie du rock. Une ontologie des artefacts et des enregistrements* (Paris: Presses Universitaires de France, 2010).

294 According to Pouivet, *Philosophie du rock*, 59, "What connoisseurs recognize immediately, when they listen to rock works, is a style of sound image. It consists of an atmosphere or a sound environment and constitutes the identity of the work. This is what a person looks for when they listen to a CD. The sound identity is based on the physical identity of the CD. The composer's intention is recorded in the sound sequence of the CD. There is no score to execute. The result can be compared to painting, when the viewer is directly in

the recording[295] (including, according to some scholars, jazz albums produced in the studio).[296] As happened with the microphone and electric amplification introduced at the end of the 1920s, recording technology in the 1950s became (as we have already pointed out) the new medium likely to significantly influence the creative act in several musical genres. As such, we can legitimately speak of a transition to the era of phonographic transmission in popular music.[297] The way in which a pop or rock album is evaluated and appreciated (magazines, blogs, fanzines, etc.) could easily support this idea: no remake, no remix, and even less any cover version will ever replace the original version of Rick Wakeman's *The Six Wives of Henry VIII* (1973) or Pink Floyd's *The Dark Side of the Moon* (1973). These are all creations where the distinctive sound is not only linked to a certain way of playing, but also to the use of special effects that are very much part of that time period (such as the sound of a cash register, or an adding machine). There was also of course the special equipment (the EMS VCS3 synthesizer, the Hammond B3 organ with its Leslie speaker and Hammond C3 for Pink Floyd; the organ of St Giles-without-Cripplegate church, the Mellotrons, and the Hohner Clavinet in the case of Rick Wakeman) and a specific analogue recording technology (Pink Floyd had use of a 16-track recorder, rather rare at the time), all quite impossible to find nowadays, where digital technology dominates. With rock works we are thus moving – just as with electronic music works – towards what can be described as a multi-instance autographic art.[298]

Saying that rock albums are artefact-recordings implies that – as with electroacoustic works – their presentation does not depend on a performative act, but on the (mere) reproduction of a trace decoded by a suitable device

---

contact with the artistic creation, without the mediation of an execution. The recordings are made as direct as a painter does."

295 If in the recent ontological debate there has been much talk of "rock works," it should be noted that the identification of a musical work with a recording artefact is not unique to rock (as observed, among others, by Sébastien Motta, "Rock Ontologie," *La vie des Idées* (2010), http://www.laviedesidees.fr/Rock-Ontologie.html, Maël Guesdom, "L'ontologie du rock de Roger Pouivet," *Volume! La revue des musiques populaires/The French journal of popular music studies*, 7/1 (2010), https://doi.org/10.4000/volume.1094): works belonging to very different genres, such as song, hip-hop, rap or film music, which are not unrelated to mass distribution, would also lend themselves to illustrating it – which once again leads us to use the more generic category of "phonographic work."

296 See Laurent Cugny, *Analyser le jazz*, 69–72. On the "debt" of jazz to 78 rpm see also Delalande, *Le son des musiques*, 52–53.

297 Olivier Julien, "'A Lucky Man Who Made the Grade': Sgt. Pepper and the Rise of a Phonographic Tradition in Twentieth-century Popular Music," in *Sgt. Pepper and the Beatles, It Was forty Years Ago Today*, ed. Olivier Julien, (Aldershot: Ashgate, 2008), 147–169.

298 Pouivet, *La philosophie du rock*, 59.

(turntable, tape recorder, etc.). According to some researchers, this possibility and its ease of listening places rock productions (along with other forms of popular culture, such as cinema, television, pulp fiction, comic strips) in the category of "mass art."[299] It has been argued that this kind of art involves an ontological innovation, insofar as the works it contains have their own mode of existence that cannot be reduced to that of works of classical art.[300] More specifically, they allow us to meet these three conditions: 1) they are multiple-instance or type-based; 2) they are produced and disseminated by mass technology (which means, among other things, that they do not in principle call for a performance); 3) they are accessible "with the least effort, virtually at first contact, to the greatest number, and even to an audience that has received no (or virtually no) training."[301]

But does a rock album actually satisfy these conditions? Rock music is a vast galaxy: while we certainly come across "easy listening" products, we also encounter (just as large) quantities of products that do not seem accessible with only little effort and whose genre requires a certain familiarity. Moreover, can we really say that, as a work of popular culture, a rock album does not call for a performance? This seems to be justified to a certain extent: a rock album is a set of tracks designed for playback, not for performance. Yet a performance was indeed necessary for it to exist in the first place as a recording artefact. How could bands like Led Zeppelin or The Rolling Stones have become what they have become, if they had never performed their own work? Unlike electronic music (at least in its "classical" version, as in Stockhausen's *Telemusik*, 1960 and 1966, for example) or acousmatic music (such as Bernard Parmegiani's *De Natura Sonorum*, 1975), rock seems to be inseparable from a performative component. Scholars who see rock music as a recording artefact imported into the popular culture market are certainly not unaware of this. In fact, they sometimes state it explicitly, as does Roger Pouivet. However, Pouivet's point of view includes a specific distinction: what rock bands have performed is, of course, rock *music*, but not really rock *works* – because these, if we look closely, coincide with recording artefacts engineered in the studio.[302]

---

299 The rock work coincides more precisely, from Pouivet's perspective, with a constructive recording that "enters the system of artistic production of popular culture" (Pouivet, *Philosophie du rock*, 13).

300 This is notably the idea of Noël Carroll, *Philosophy of Mass Art* (Oxford: Clarendon, 1998) and Roger Pouivet, *L'œuvre d'art à l'âge de sa mondialisation, une ontologie de l'art de masse* (Bruxelles: La lettre volée, 2003).

301 Pouivet, *L'œuvre d'art à l'âge de sa mondialisation*, 21.

302 Pouivet, *La philosophie du rock*, 66–67.

The question can be further developed on the basis of two issues: first, the connotations or morphological characteristics of what we can perceive in a constructive recording and second, the work of the musicians on stage. Let us start with the first issue. From an ontological point of view, a constructive recording should not be considered as simply a means of access to the work, but – in terms of the Peircien type/token distinction – as a true token of the type/work. In other words, when listening to this kind of artefact, Pouivet observes, it should not be necessary to intentionally attend to something else (we don't expect that the recording has any transparency): "we listen to what we hear and nothing else, nothing that is given to listening and to which we must intentionally attend."[303] This remark is fundamentally correct, but in our opinion it contains an ambiguity that needs to be clarified if misunderstandings are to be avoided. This is because the idea of "not intentionally attending to anything else" might very well lead us to a kind of acousmatic listening: that is, a way of listening where we only focus on the dynamic properties of the sound objects (their gestural and textural morphology) without conscious reference to the original sound source.[304] If we imply this meaning, we will therefore have to recognize that it is applicable to electroacoustic music, but that it is certainly less relevant in the case of rock. The idea that a Pink Floyd album can be considered fundamentally as an electronic or an acousmatic work is somewhat misguided: because in reality when we listen to it, however attentive we may be to the sound dynamics and morphology, we are inclined to perceive its real physically gestural content (something that is absent, by definition, from an acousmatic perspective). Let us consider the performances of instrumental virtuosos (such as Eddie van Halen, Jimi Hendrix and Rick Wakeman, whom we have already mentioned): we no doubt tend to consider them as *real* performances that we perceive *through* the medium of recording. In other words, if a recording in rock music is not supposed to be a faithful reproduction of a performance, it still constitutes a representation of it.[305]

---

303 Pouivet, "La triple ontologie des deux sortes d'enregistrements musicaux," 171.

304 The idea of "acousmatic listening," introduced by Pierre Schaeffer, *Treatise on Musical Objects. An Essay across Disciplines*, trans. Christine North and John Dack (Oakland: University of California Press, 2017), 69 (1st edition in French: 1966), was fundamental to the activities of the Groupe de recherches musicales (GRM), founded in Paris by the same composer.

305 See Gracyk, *Rhythm and Noise*, 44. More generally, as Bernard Sève noted, all music produced with instruments, whether recorded or not, is received in an oscillation between "horizontal" and a "vertical" listening; Bernard Sève, *L'instrument de musique* (Paris, Seuil, 2013), 280.

What can we deduce from this? First of all, that it is not appropriate to consider the functioning of all phonographic works as homogeneous: there is music made in the studio which, more than other sorts, appeals to the idea of performance. But what kind of performance is it, exactly? In the studio we have several possibilities that a concert situation is unable to offer: we can do as many takes as necessary until we get the result we want; we can superimpose the recording of what we have played over other takes to obtain a particular effect; we can filter, play the tape backwards, mix it with pre-recorded sounds ... in short, the whole range of possible modifications that a cult album like *Sgt. Pepper's Lonely Hearts Club Band* (and countless albums produced after it in rock history) has so clearly and masterfully demonstrated. How can we consider the performance that will be presented to us in such a recording? As we pointed out in the first part, we have roughly two choices: to deny that such an act has the status of a musical performance or to give it a special status. If Roger Pouivet defended the first option,[306] Stephen Davies opted for the second:[307] with certain works made in the studio, we should instead speak of "studio performance," that is to say, a performance that is explicitly oriented towards the production of a recording artefact, and which is therefore often partial, reiterative at will, and involving all the possibilities of editing, filtering and sound engineering that we have just mentioned. In short, a performance that remains conceptually distinct from the ordinary performance that musicians make on stage, characterized by a fundamental temporal irreversibility. This second option seems to be more convincing from the point of view of both production and reception. We need now to see why.

As far as the production criteria are concerned, it may well be that in some cases, such as techno or electro music, but also all the productions that today can be made with a laptop and commonly available software,[308] the track is finalized without there being strictly any performance; but in many other situations, a performative act is necessary – as happens, say, in the production of a Mark Knopfler album, an Edoardo Bennato song or a soundtrack by Ennio Morricone. In these cases, the musicians can certainly rehearse their performance, which can then be edited or modified to make a good phonographic product; but such editing work cannot entirely replace their act, which generally remains very recognizable (think of the timbre and expressiveness

306 Pouivet, *Philosophie du rock*, 65.
307 Davies, *Musical Works and Performances*, 34–36.
308 Like "Logic-pro" or "Garage band" (on Apple devices).

of a voice,[309] the highly personal "magic" of a groove, etc.). Let us note that this act then assumes a value that is both performative and creative: in fact, the performance (no matter whether it is improvised or has been prepared in advance) ends up constituting, if not the whole work, at least one of its parts. This is a good point which we can use to answer a question we asked in the introduction to this essay: if Clare Torry was right to claim copyright for her improvised performance at Abbey Road Studios in one of the recording sessions for the album *The Dark Side of the Moon*, it is because such a performance is indeed part of the work – at least insofar as we assume that the album is a phonographic work and not a recording that contains the "simple" document of a performance. So, in this case, an improvised performance is likely to be part of the construction of the musical work.

The specific character of a "studio performance" also appears justified if we consider the most common ways of listening to it or how it is represented to us. When we listen to a rock album, we are usually inclined to consider (and even welcome) solutions that would be inappropriate when listening to a record with music by Beethoven or Brahms: the voice of a single singer multiplied (or over-recorded) to the point of becoming a lush homorhythmic polyphony, the echo repetition of a word that gradually deteriorates acoustically until it turns into the barking of a dog,[310] a performance that ends with the ubiquitous "fade out," etc. All these possibilities, common in the fields of pop or rock, would seem extravagant when listening to a work based on a score (except, of course, in the case of so-called mixed music works, where the sound of acoustic instruments is added to the electronic sounds, which are recorded or produced in real time – we will come back to this later). It therefore seems correct to say that while the making of a phonographic work may, in some cases, involve a real performance, in its normative status it integrates as a matter of principle the idea that Davies has called a "virtual performance,"[311] i.e. a performance including sound possibilities that can (legitimately) take us beyond the limits of reality.[312]

309 A good example of this can be found in the recorded voice of the Italian "cantautori"; on the phonographic singularity of Fabrizio De André's voice, see Franco Fabbri, *L'ascolto tabù. Le musiche nello scontro globale* (Milano: Il Saggiatore, 2017), 216–222.

310 See Pink Floyd, "Dogs," second track in the *Animals* album (Harvest and Columbia, 1977).

311 Davies, *Themes in the Philosophy of Music*, 37.

312 These limitations are present, on the contrary, in the case of what Davies calls a "simulated performance" (*Themes in the Philosophy of Music*, 38). This is what sometimes happens in the studio recording of score-based works: you take the best parts of several performances and you get a result that, without corresponding to a single real event simulates it as much as possible.

It is therefore worth clarifying what is involved in adopting the category of "constructive recording" in the case of rock music. The idea of limiting ourselves to listening to what we hear "without intentionally attending to something else" may be misleading if it implies that we are not focusing on an actual gesture or action that would cause it. On the other hand, the same remark is correct in another sense, if it is formally stated as follows: *only the record* (and not a unit that pre-exists it) *is supposed to bring together all the aesthetic properties of the work* (which could somehow be considered as the result of a performative act "enhanced," so to speak, by studio technologies). As a complete entity, a phonographic work does not in fact exist until the master recording is finalized. It is therefore pointless to ensure that the recording maintains its conformity to a (pre-existing) type; but it should be stressed that this does not exclude the idea that the recording may contain traces of performances that we consider real or effective, and in relation to which it certainly also functions in part as a document.[313] Could we make the same judgment on a Pink Floyd record if we knew that the band members did not play what we hear, and that even the voices were not theirs?

That thought seems to muddy the waters of what was shaping up to be a (simple) problem of choice between two opposing options. In truth, it shows that the main question is not whether to refer – or not to refer at all – to something other than the recording itself, but rather what meaning we are willing to give to such a recording: that is, whether we are willing to recognize it (categorically) as an end or as a (mere) means. But it also highlights the need not to overlook some important differences that can be identified within the class of phonographic works.

Let us turn to the second issue mentioned, i.e. the work as it appears on the stage. Let us start again from the very clear position that Roger Pouivet has on this subject: what the musicians do on the stage is "rock music," not "rock works"; because what they play on such occasions are their *songs*, not properly their *works*[314] – where the first term refers, in Davies' terms, to ontologically *thin* structures (composed of a melodic-harmonic structure and possibly a text), while the second refers to the ontologically *thick* entities (thick to the point of being essentially unalterable) that are the recording artefacts. According to Pouivet, this is not only true for albums where the recording is

313 Theodore Gracyk further reflected on the difficulties of classifying rock works from a single recording category. See "Documentation and Transformation in Musical Recordings," in *Recorded Music. Philosophical and Critical Reflections*, ed. Mine Doğantan-Dack (London: Middlesex University Press, 2008), 61–81.

314 Pouivet, *Philosophie du rock*, 67.

based on sophisticated construction techniques (as in the examples we have already mentioned), but also for folk or country music records where the recording is made in a single take. Bob Dylan's *John Wesley Harding*, recorded in 1967, is particularly revealing in this regard, as it has "a very special sound. It is a property of the recording, much more than of what is recorded."[315] Thus, if Dylan – or any other musician – were to decide to cover this album in concert, he could not perform the work (fixed once and for all on the record): he could only cover the songs.

Now, it is true that what a musician can cover in concert is only part of what he has achieved in the studio. It is also possible to decide to conventionally call this part "song" (although the term can be a source of misunderstanding); on the other hand, it seems inappropriate to emphasize the difference between such a structure and the complete work, or to take it as a fundamental opposition. The song (or the ontologically thin sound structure) is by no means an element that can be considered secondary or external to the unity of the work: on the contrary, it usually constitutes a central core of it. One might say that it is a matter of opinion: sometimes a sound or a sound image seems somehow more important than a melodic or harmonic structure (and which explains the success of a rock production); but generally the situation is not so relative. A DJ who plays a song by Daft Punk or Albano Carrisi during a party in a public place without paying for the digital license to use such songs can be fined by the copyright collection authorities (such as the Performing Rights Society in the UK), and a musical group that took the liberty to cover these songs and present them in their own arrangement without having paid for the same license may also be fined: this band could certainly not defend themselves by saying that they did not really cover the *work* of Albano or Daft Punk! Whatever the orchestration, the (simple) fact of adopting the melodic-harmonic structure and the text seems enough to make it a cover of the work. Is this only proof that the laws are open to improvement and that they can be remarkably imprecise? Perhaps. But we think rather that when a work manifests a well-defined melodic and harmonic structure, this structure generally constitutes a crucial element of its identity. One could say that it presents itself, to use Ingarden's terminology in our way, as one of its "strata."[316] And to be even more precise, a basic stratum, since we expect to find some of the salient aesthetic properties in it. A rock band that would be unable to present it on stage would be more the exception than the rule. It would therefore be somewhat wrong to say that what that band produces at that point in time does not really give us

315 Pouivet, *Philosophie du rock*, 65.
316 Ingarden, *The Work of Music and the Problem of Its Identity*, 52.

access to the work: more reasonably, it will give us access to one or more of its most distinctive strata.

Perhaps a kind of ontology "by concentric circles," similar to the one Bernard Sève conceived to explain the implementation of works based on scores,[317] should be used to clarify this situation: if in rock and pop music we think in terms of ontological "density," we would say that the phonographic work exists "fully" in the master recording, whereas the performances we can hear in concert only make it exist in a reduced form. Thus, if we think of its "full" form as located in the centre, its "diminished" or reduced forms become increasingly peripheral circles. We will thus go from a version closer to the recording, capable of better restoring the properties of the work (originally phonographic) to a version so impoverished that it becomes "a lifeless and untruthful diagram or extract."[318] This explanation – a very functional one in the case of the work based on the score – should nevertheless take into account an additional variable. If, in a stage performance, the work has fewer aspects than its full phonographic version, it may also have some additional aspects: unexpected solos, arrangements that enhance its dynamism, light effects and a spectacle-like dimension that make it more vibrant. Let us imagine we want to present a hit by Abba on stage: *The Winner Takes it All*, (published as a single and on the *Super Trouper* album in 1980). The group Abba no longer appears on stage (except on very rare occasions). Proposing the original record or its remastering would be useless: what the public expects is its presentation in a show; the song will be adapted by what is called a tribute band to the new listening situation (with a certain arrangement, new voices, a new show, etc.). Since it will seek to respect a certain structural similarity with the original, this performance will meet a different identification criterion and different modes of transmission (based on the model of a sample taken as an example and to which variations are applied). That brings us closer to the criteria and kind of normativity that characterizes oral works. One might say that these additions are external to its being; which is probably true if we take the artefact-recording as a reference for the fullness of its existence. It is no less true, however, that on the stage pop and rock works seem to assume another existence, and certainly also respond to another normativity.

Let us consider once more the case of covers (or what in France are called *reprises*). This phenomenon, which is very widespread and has increased further with diffusion on digital platforms and social media, concerns several musical genres and is found in several forms, ranging from adaptation

317 Sève, *L'instrument de musique*, 329–335.
318 Sève, *L'instrument de musique*, 334.

to arrangement to parody. Now, as we have just seen, what is included in a cover is a stratum of the work whose centrality justifies protection by copyright laws. Could we consider this recording as the document of a performance of the original work? That would not be appropriate. A cover is usually recorded in the studio: we can expect it to meet to the normativity of phonographic works. Indeed, the way in which the copyright laws of several countries consider covers largely confirms this expectation. Thus, for example, the Nomadi's version of a song such as "In morte di S. F.,"[319] better known as "Canzone per un'amica," by the Italian singer/songwriter Francesco Guccini, will be legally considered a new phonographic work, even though it is based on the melodic-harmonic structure of the previous song (which justifies Nomadi's payment of rights to Guccini).[320] Perhaps we can explain it this way: once imported into a new phonographic construction, the original stratum (the song) gives life to what is presented as a new work, whose authorship is no longer attributed to the same author.

To sum up: a cover is to be considered as a work to which the author of the original song – on which it is based – has no rights.[321] This is to some extent confirmed by the public's attitude towards this kind of product: what is appreciated in a cover is the way in which the musicians have "appropriated" what they have found in the recording – rather than merely performing it as faithfully as possible (even though these cases also exist and have become quite numerous today)[322] – in order to produce a new original recording. In short, the legal status of a cover conforms to its ontological status, which is that of a phonographic work.

If in rock and pop the work consists of a recording-artefact, we must not lose sight of the fact that one of its layers is made up of a thinner musical structure: the song. We are inclined to think that such structure was generally conceived not only to form the basis of the recording artefact, but also to be covered. Indeed, when he sang and recorded his own songs, Dylan could perfectly well have imagined that someone else would one day sing them

319 The second track on the *Folk Beat* album n. 1 (for the "La voce del padrone" label), 1967.

320 It is interesting to note that in France, a song can be covered without the author's prior authorization: provided that the author is explicitly mentioned in the credits, that the work is covered in a way that conforms to the original version (in particular the title, the text and the melodic structure) and that the performing rights are paid and paid back to the author via the rights collection organization.

321 Provided, as we have just seen, that the author of the cover has paid the performing rights.

322 This is the case of "tribute bands" such as the Australian Pink Floyd (http://www.aussiefloyd.com/), who have become famous for their ability to reproduce live the sound nuances of the British band's original albums.

(especially if that someone else's name was Joan Baez!). In fact, many have covered and will continue to cover Dylan's songs; and the same fate fortunately concerns today the songs of most of the bands that have made rock history, including the Beatles the Eagles, Genesis, etc. But what conclusion should we draw from this? Does rock have a double life?

We think so. Rock exists in the form of works that consist of artefacts-recordings; at the same time, and to no lesser extent, it exists in the form of performances that largely adopt one of the layers of these to function in other ways. These include the features that we have considered typical of oral works. Thus, for example, "Yesterday" – one of the most covered hits in the world according to the Rolling Stone magazine, – is an ontologically dense phonographic work that, in a strict sense, only a DJ – and not a musical group – would be able to reproduce in its entirety. This same work, or one of its strata, can, however, form not only the basis of a concert performance, but also the main source of inspiration for another phonographic work, with its own aesthetic qualities. Moreover, this same work may give rise, on stage, to performances that also adopt one of its strata (comprising its title, text and a recognizable part of its melodic and harmonic outline) and, in fact, make it work like an oral work. Indeed the work on stage obeys its own rules: variations, solos, changes of key or orchestration are welcome, insofar as it is not really a question of instantiating all the details fixed on disc. This could confer a new relevance to the idea of a new or "second orality," sometimes employed in jazz and pop, and shows more particularly the fact that musicians tend to "bypass" the act of writing in order to find, via recording, a more direct mode of fixing and transmitting their ideas: in fact, the ontological thickness of the trace (constituted by the recording), far from discouraging the impulse of variation, seems in some way to favour it. In other words, variation and arrangement are constantly at work precisely in cultures where the fixation and diffusion of the work (as in rock and pop music) is ensured by the record.

The principle of transition from one normative system to another, intrinsic to most rock and pop music, assumes a different meaning in the case of traditional music based on the principle of oral transmission. Let us return again to the example of the *canto a tenores* from the Sardinian tradition: its recording and dissemination on YouTube will not automatically transform it into a phonographic work, just as its transcription will not transform it into a notated work. If the trace is originally oral, the score and the recording will have no normative value (although they can certainly establish certain possibilities of performance). In this musical culture, if we find traces that are valid as patterns subject to local variations, we think of them as being the (documentary) recording of a (singular) performance of an oral work; if it is only one of the possible conjunctural realizations of a set of fixed parameters, we think of it as being an (equally documentary) recording of an improvisation.

A different case is the productions of what is conventionally known as "world music." Largely based on models borrowed from traditional music, they often rely on a sound and a performance style that establishes the original "stamp" or hallmark of a band or a musician. The imperative of authenticity that accompanies the recording of traditional music, whose value is documentary, changes its meaning here:[323] while inspired by the oral tradition of the *fado*, an album such as "Ainda" (1995, soundtrack of the film "Lisbon Story") by the Portuguese group *Madredeus* is above all an original phonographic creation, associated with a specific sound image. Eminently constructive, this recording is nevertheless supposed to maintain – as in the case of rock – a documentary value in relation to the performative act carried out by the musicians. A similar observation could be made for the productions of the Tunisian *oud* player Anouar Brahem, which are explicitly based on the crossover between the improvisational practices of the *maquam* and the rhythms and sounds of jazz. Indeed, if these sorts of music are based on improvisational practices, they are clearly fixed in their connotations on recordings made in the studio, which have a well-defined and, as it were, unalterable performativity and sound balance. One could certainly imagine that one day musicians will play this music based on the scores that Brahem could have composed; but at present they are presented as works that respond above all to a normativity that is that of phonographic works – whose live presentation concerns, as we have seen, one of its main strata.

The class of phonographic works is actually populated by examples that manifest different degrees of ontological complexity and which adopt different kinds of enactment. A "classical" work such as Karlheinz Stockhausen's *Gesang der Jünglinge* (1955–56), based entirely on the fusion of electronic sounds and human voices, explicitly displays its phonographic status: it was conceived as a master recording and, as such, is usually broadcast (and sometimes reproduced in concert). Of course, we could always design a system to transcribe it:[324] but, once again, the result will appear devoid of normative value. The discourse changes, on the other hand, when mixed works are addressed: if, in

323 See Sandrine Darsel, "Musique et enregistrement. Une exploration goodmanienne des musiques du monde," in *Ontologie musicale: perspectives et débats*, ed. Alessandro Arbo and Marcello Ruta, (Paris: Hermann, 2014), 185–203.

324 As in the "aural score" developed by Carl Bergstroem-Nielsen: https://www.youtube.com/watch?v=s7HD-95knVQ.

some aspects, their functioning is phonographic, in others it responds plainly to the normativity of notated works, since it provides for a score whose interpretation is entrusted to a performer. Take a classic of the genre such as Bruno Maderna's *Musica su due dimensioni* (1952). The work is entirely based on the dialogue between a flute and the magnetic tape and is one of the first mixed pieces in the electroacoustic repertoire. On the one hand there is the tape, realized at the "Studio di Fonologia" of the Radio of Milan, and made up of flute and electronic sounds; on the other hand there is the flute part, a score that nevertheless leaves the performer a great deal of freedom (they can choose the order of the phrases, the tempo, the dynamics and the instrumental techniques, in order to create an effective polyphony with the recorded part). For competent listeners, it is therefore a notated work (i.e. a work responding to the normativity of notated works) – even if it leaves a lot of freedom to the musician and includes a recorded part. If we listen to a recording of this work, it will therefore be a documentary type of recording (even if it includes, in this act of documentation, a constructive recording).

Another case is music that uses live electronics. Most of the time, these are productions whose status lies between two poles, that of free improvisation and that of the work linked to previously fixed sound structure. Since the trace of such a structure is fixed electronically, one would be tempted to classify them as phonographic works. This is, however, not at all obvious, since these works make explicit use of performative acts – normally made possible by specific interfaces. In this sense, it seems more correct to consider them as notated works, whose notation has the distinctive feature of being constituted by the instantaneous input of a code into an electronic device.

Ultimately, it is important to identify how the artefact functions in its production and reception contexts. In the avant-garde music of the last century, it is not uncommon to come across works that the composer wanted to evolve over time, sometimes changing their status. This is the case of *Hymnen*, which was realized by Karlheinz Stockhausen in the Electronic Music Studio of the Westdeutscher Rundfunk (WDR) in Cologne in 1966–67 and then revived in 1969. This work originally consisted of recordings of various national anthems that were edited and modified electronically. However, it exists in three versions, the first of which consists of a mix of electronic music and *musique concrète*, the second of electronic music with solo musicians and the third for orchestra only. One could say here that the work has evolved (in accordance with the composer's own intentions) or that it has somehow "migrated" from one ontological status to another: while the first version is unquestionably a phonographic work, the second is an example of mixed music, while the third is clearly a notated work.

The difference between these types of works may seem even clearer if we consider their identity from a legal point of view. There is a famous case that could help us to show this. In 1992, the Italian singer and composer Albano Carrisi filed a complaint against Michael Jackson, claiming that with "Will You Be There," a 1991 hit from Jackson's album *Dangerous*, the King of Pop had plagiarized one of his songs, "I Cigni di Balaka" ("The Swans of Balaka"), which dates from 1987 and was released in the United States in 1989. In 1995, a judge in the Rome court[325] ruled that Jackson had indeed plagiarized Albano's song; as a result, the album had to be withdrawn from sale in Italy, and a request was made to prevent any further distribution of the work in any form whatsoever. Both songs can now be easily found on social media: the reader will be able to form their own idea of what appears to be a morphological (real and effective) resemblance. However, the courts had not yet had their last word. In fact, Jackson's lawyers considered the court's finding to be unfounded: on the one hand, because it was issued by a judge who was considered incompetent in musical subjects; on the other hand, because it was contrary to the conclusions of experts who proved that the two songs had both been inspired by the melodic structure of another pre-existing song: "Bless You For Being An Angel" (1939) by the Ink Spots, a vocal band of African-American origin famous in the 30s and 40s. Neither of the two songs could therefore be considered original. What is more, the Ink Spots' song could not claim to be entirely original either: the same band (which by the way had not registered copyrights) took inspiration from a traditional Native American song. The accusation of plagiarism thus could not be founded for any of these songs.

This case is interesting in many ways. It shows to what extent in pop music imitation and copying often take the lion's share (and also how much this genre is inspired by traditional music). Moreover, it draws attention to a discontinuity between artefacts for which one can (legally) claim authorship – and thus receive copyright – and artefacts for which this claim is not justified. One would be tempted to say that what is really at stake is the distinction between what presents itself as a work and what, legally, cannot claim that title. Such a distinction is however meaningless in the light of our typology, which also includes oral works. Indeed, if the connotations of Amerindian song are not attributable to an author, they are clearly identifiable as part of the sound structure of that song: a song associated with a culture, a group or a community that has appropriated it or that can (or could) recognize itself in it. Certainly, nothing is more common, when entering a traditional musical

325 More precisely, the judge of the first civil section of the Court of Rome, Domenico Bonaccorsi.

culture, than to encounter borrowings, mixtures or crossovers of music from other cultures or origins. In fact, in circumstances that we do not know, but that it is sometimes possible to reconstruct, a civilization or a human group appropriates a song: it recognizes a musical unity in its morphology that is linked to its own cultural identity. In our opinion, this condition is sufficient for the song to be considered as an oral work that bears the "mark" of this human group, as it is that group (or some members of that group), and not another, that has indicated it. The identity of such a song is ontological: if the legal claim of its intellectual property has no *raison d'être* – as long as it is not attributable to a particular subject or individual – it is nonetheless true that this song is for us clearly linked to a culture and a tradition that surrounded its origin. What does the dispute between Carrisi and Jackson ultimately show? That in the difference – established by law – between a musical work that can claim copyright and a piece of traditional music for which these rights cannot be claimed lies the (most fundamental) difference in ontological status between a phonographic (or notated) musical work and an oral musical work.

There are actually important differences between the way musical plagiarism is dealt with from a legal and an ontological point of view. In legal proceedings many aspects have nothing or little to do with the comparison of artistic or musical elements: "issues related to the right to file a complaint, the definition of the object of legal protection, the burden of proof and so on."[326] More crucially, one could observe that, while for ontology objective and categorical comparison constitutes the main criterion for the identification of the properties of the artefact in question, such a criterion does not assume the same role in the legal sphere. Copyright law tends to safeguard a certain degree of generality and subjectivity, leaving the decision on the case to the person (rather than the application of an objective criterion).[327] Besides, more than founding the judgement on the identification of musical properties, for the courts it is a question of entrusting it to an "overall impression" or an "aesthetic experience," and not necessarily informed by specific knowledge.

As far as such a view can be legally well-founded, however, this last remark does not seem to me to be conclusive. Although the need to preserve a margin of freedom for the person who decides is understandable, I would like to suggest that the identification of the main qualities of the work (and of its ontological status) offers those who judge some elements to make their judgement more sound, especially when it is founded on what (in this context) can be called an "aesthetic experience." After all, such an experience, as well as

326 Döhl, "Per un campo di dibattito interdisciplinare," 48.
327 Döhl, "Per un campo di dibattito interdisciplinare," 58.

the general perception of any work of art, is largely mediated by concepts and categories:[328] being aware of which of these are valid in a given context can certainly do no harm to the judge!

We can still dwell on the interesting case of phonographic works that combine music and image. When this combination is not purely functional or subsequent to the constitution of the work, it may assume a particular significance. Let us take as an example the "video opera" *An Index of Metals* (2003), with music by Fausto Romitelli, text by Kenka Lekovich and video realized by Paolo Pachini and Leonardo Romoli. The music calls for an interpretation of a finely written instrumental and vocal score that involves improvised parts (*ad lib* cadenzas entrusted to the musicians), electronic sounds fixed on a medium and samplings from Pink Floyd and Pansonic records. What exactly is the identity of this work? First of all, it can be said that it is a mixed work, where the mixing explicitly includes musical quotations and a visual (artistic) dimension. This is not exceptional in itself: there is certainly no lack of musical quotations in the music of the past; moreover, was not the opera originally a mix of music, text and images or music, text and stage? But if we put aside the quotations (which are in fact reduced to short sound borrowings), there is a significant difference. Unlike a musical drama by Wagner or Puccini – which can be represented with different scenographies – *An Index of Metals* results from the meeting of music and a video *fixed on a medium*: it is a *video-phonographic* musical work and not simply a phonographic one (changing the images here would in fact mean ignoring the ontological status of the work).[329]

These examples confirm that the most decisive criterion for understanding what type of work is at stake lies in observing how it is considered (and judged) in the contexts of its reception. Reconstructing the contexts in which music is received is certainly not an easy task.[330] It is not always simple to establish who are the most competent judges of a certain musical genre and, if need be,

---

328 As amply demonstrated in Kendall Walton's classic essay, "Categories of Art," *The Philosophical Review* 79/3 (1970): 334–367.

329 This operation is of course still possible, and it was offered in concert by the American ensemble "Talea." In the United States, for the *première* of *An Index of Metals* (2011), the music was coupled with a new video (made only for this production). In this case we will then say that we are not dealing with a new interpretation of the work, but, up to a certain point, with a new work (which would have owed a large artistic debt to the previous production: *An Index of Metals 2.0*, with new aesthetic properties, due to a different interplay between image and music).

330 If evaluation is a complex language game in which, as Wittgenstein pointed out, a whole culture is reflected, we will certainly not lack subjects for observation: we will at least need to know who formulates the judgement, in what circumstances, how, and with reference to which object in particular; see Ludwig Wittgenstein, *Lectures and Conversations*

to resolve any conflicts of opinion that may arise between them. It should also be noted that the reception contexts for most music today are much less "compartmentalized" than in the past: the same work can easily function within different contexts of evaluation.[331] These same contexts are also likely to vary over time. Finally, we may also have to resolve conflicts between what seems to be suggested by the production context and the reception contexts: will it always be reasonable to support the latter?

These are certainly serious difficulties but not insurmountable. The variability of our ways of categorizing the world is not necessarily an obstacle: on the contrary, it should be a stimulus for studying the functioning of these social objects that we call musical works. On the other hand, we need to be aware that only careful observation will enable us to grasp the ontological status and properties of the artefact in question. We should not believe that their functioning can be defined once and for all: it is possible that one day changes may occur, whether because of a change in the capacities of listeners in new contexts of reception, or because of a technical, technological or instrumental innovation likely to modify our ways of experiencing them. At the same time, in this changing situation, there are stages or steps that show a certain level of stability and become objectively identifiable; and it is on these very steps that an ontological analysis of musical artefacts has every interest in focusing its attention.

For example, today we can easily identify a Bach cello suite when played on a modern cello; however, if someone were to argue that its performance with a sampler is a correct instance of the work, we might be more confused. The fact that such a judgment may vary over time does not compromise the stability of the identification criteria that are held to be valid in a certain context and at a certain time. This principle applies not only to musical works, but also to all forms of artistic expression. We need only think of the extent to which today we generally identify a film on the basis of a videogram and audiogram that does not necessarily use the voices of the actors; in other words, a film that has been dubbed or subtitled remains for us *the same film* (and not an adaptation or a new version of the original film), even if we admit that our experience of it may be different (and sometimes even not in a negligible way). While there is no guarantee that a change in audience attention will not one day alter this

on Aesthetics, Psychology and Religious Belief, ed. Cyril Barrett (Berkeley and Los Angeles: University of California Press, 1967), 8.

331 Romitelli's music could still be a good example: judging by the comments on the videos posted on YouTube, the contexts of evaluation of this composer's works is obviously broader than that of so-called "contemporary" music: it often includes an audience more familiar with rock and techno than with Ligeti or spectralism.

situation, we can at least say that it is confirmed at some point by our most common ways of relating to such artefacts.

3.5 *Digital Environments*

The digital transition is without a doubt one of the phenomena that has most marked the systems of production, distribution and reception of music in the last twenty years. Several emerging phenomena are directly related to it, including the increasingly frequent use of samplers and sampling techniques, the generalization of multimedia productions, the increase in self-production and interactivity, and the hybridization of genres. One may legitimately wonder whether these phenomena, sometimes grouped together under the expression "digital revolution in music"[332] or "numerimorphosis"[333] have also had repercussions on the ontological status of works, and if so, which ones. In the final part of our essay we will attempt to answer this question by focusing on the aspects that have attracted the most attention from scholars.

One could already begin by asking whether the entry into cyberspace might not have to some extent favoured forms of de-contextualization likely to undermine or, more or less indirectly, weaken the very existence of the musical works. At the end of the 1930s, Adorno had pointed out the phenomenon of a regression in listening.[334] The way in which musical works (classical, rock or pop) are presented today on streaming sites, which attract listeners eager for instant satisfaction, runs the risk of amplifying this phenomenon: the work is fragmented and "projected" towards fragmentary and isolated listening. We have seen to what extent the identification of its properties depends on the presence of certain capacities in listeners. A glance at the comments accompanying the music videos posted on YouTube would be enough to make us realize that, more often than not, they are spoken about, commented on or judged too hastily, sketchily and, in the end, inappropriately. It doesn't matter, one might say: everyone is now free to express themselves and to do so publicly; it's part of the social media game. And if one once had to listen to the radio (where works were often presented) or buy a record (which usually

332 See Harry Lehmann, *Die digitale Revolution der Musik. Eine Musikphilosophie* (Mainz: Schott Music, 2012).

333 Fabien Grandjon and Clément Combes, "Digitamorphosis of Music Consumption Practices: The Case of Young Music Lovers," *French Cultural Studies*, 20, n. 3 (2009), 287–314; Philippe Le Guern, "Introduction," in *Où va la musique? Numérimorphose et nouvelles expériences d'écoute*, ed. Philippe Le Guern (Paris: Presses des Mines, 2016), 13–45.

334 Theodor Wiesengrund Adorno, "On the Fetish-Character in Music and the Regression of Listening," in Theodor Wiesengrund Adorno, *Essays on Music*, ed. Richard Leppert, trans. Susan Gillespie (Berkeley & Los Angeles: University of California Press, 2002), 288–317.

contained a minimum of condensed contextual information in the booklet), nowadays anyone, whether out of simple curiosity or on the recommendation of an algorithm, can listen to and comment – even if only with a basic "like" or "dislike" – on works or performances of which he or she knows absolutely nothing. The main streaming sites will limit themselves to offering the disc cover and very little additional information. A "naive listener," unable to identify the salient features of what they are listening to, will thus be highly inclined to make categorical errors and to make inappropriate judgements. The repetition and rapid diffusion of these errors (made possible by digital platforms) may help to confuse the original normativity of the work, and sometimes even to dilute it in a more generic and confused mode of listening. One might then wonder whether we should continue to speak of transformations in the historical time of the same work, or of the birth of a new phenomenon. It is to be feared that one day a majority of listeners will be unable to correctly identify the aesthetic properties of musical works: these will then end up being lost in a flow of music without quality, just like "muzak."[335] In addition, their constant availability could cause a loss of their symbolic value and of the rituality that once accompanied them.[336]

These tendencies conceal dangers that must be taken seriously; to assert, however, that they will end up compromising the very existence of musical works seems excessive to us. A counter-argument to the assumption of the disappearance of the conditions necessary for the recognition of the aesthetic properties of works could be the following: if the contemporary listener wants to know who composed a song (or the place and time of its composition), they now have at their disposal highly effective tools; in other words, it is possible to obtain information about it in a remarkably short period of time. After all, the web provides us with incomparably more powerful tools for finding information than the encyclopaedias used to offer us. However, information is not necessarily synonymous with knowledge: between the two is the question of the reliability of the sources – reliability that can only be ensured with a sufficiently developed critical eye. The survival of the conditions that enable us to identify the salient properties of musical works depends on training or education in the use of these same tools that have taken them away from their original contexts. In spite of everything, we tend to think that this constitutes an important innovation compared to the era of traditional media: radio and

335 A remark made by Davies, *Themes*, 46. On the origins and development of Muzak in the 20th century, see Juliette Volcler, *Contrôle. Comment s'inventa l'art de la manipulation sonore* (Paris: Cité de la musique/Philarmonie de Paris, 2017), 45–71.

336 Le Guern, "Introduction," 30.

television certainly offered us a lot of information; but the web, which from its first version considerably weakened the distinction between the means of communication and the means of recording,[337] offers us much more and whose access is free.

Another issue often raised when talking about the transformation of musical works on the web is the so-called "dematerialisation of media." We have passed from the age when we made copies (from disc to MP3 files, which still applies to devices such as the iPod)[338] to the age of streaming, where music, it has often been [illegible] floats on the cloud.[339] It is a migration that has given it a new ubiquity, and has allowed the fulfilment of the prophecy of permanent availability of its works formulated by Valéry, as we have recalled, almost 90 years earlier.[340] We are sorely tempted to suspect the emergence of an ontological change. Is such a deduction correct?

As social entities, as we have seen, works depend on the fixing of a trace – which, in turn, needs a physical medium. The fact that the latter coincides with local hard-drives or central databases has certainly had decisive consequences on a mediological level,[341] as well as on the reconfiguration of the "socio-technical listening devices",[342] and on the legal and economic levels. It should be remembered that a digital file is a very different 'thing' from a record: in economics, it is considered a "non-rival resource," because its use by one person does not limit the use that another could make of it.[343] This change has shaken up the music market and generated new consumer practices, which are increasingly difficult to regulate legally.[344] In addition, the possi-

337 Maurizio Ferraris, *Mobilitazione totale* (Roma and Bari: Laterza, 2015), 67.

338 See Ernesto Assante, *Copio, dunque sono. La rivoluzione elettronica che ha cambiato la musica* (Roma: Coniglio Editore, 2009).

339 Joseph Ghosn, *Musiques numériques. Essai sur la vie nomade de la musique* (Paris: Seuil, 2013), 155.

340 Valéry, "La conquête de l'ubiquité," 1283.

341 See Vincent Tiffon, "Pour une médiologie musicale comme mode original de connaissance," *Filigrane* 1 (2005), 122–123.

342 Paolo Magaudda, *Oggetti da ascoltare. Hifi, iPod e consumo delle tecnologie musicali* (Bologna, il Mulino, 2012), 173; François Debruyne, "Environnements numériques de l'écoute et culture publique. Vers de nouvelles formes de domestication de l'expérience musicale?" in *Où va la musique? Numérimorphose et nouvelles expériences d'écoute*, ed. Philippe Le Guern (Paris: Presses des Mines, 2016), 81–91.

343 See Mark Katz, *Capturing Sound: How Technology Has Changed Music* (Berkeley and Los Angeles: University of California Press, 2010), 183.

344 Ghosn, *Musiques numériques*, 81; Florence Icard and Marianne Serfaty, "Études et recherche à la Hadopi: retour d'expérience sur l'observation des pratiques culturelles dématérialisées," in *En quête de musique. Questions de méthode à l'ère de la numérimorphose*, ed. Philippe Le Guern, 145–163 (Paris: Hermann, 2017).

bility of "freeing" local hard-drives and making it increasingly easy to access music streaming platforms has changed our listening habits, exposing us to entirely new systems of promotion and selection.

To assert that these phenomena testify to an ontological change in the works, on the other hand, seems to us rather dubious – and even, to tell the truth, erroneous. Let us note first of all that what we call "demateralisation" concerns the *medium* and not the *trace* (to think otherwise would be a bit like believing that paying for something using a contactless credit card is not a real payment because we don't see the money). Let us then specify that, even for the media, we are not dealing with a total dematerialisation: if the trace is not present in the local memories, it is certainly present in the electrical charges of the semiconductors of the central servers.[345] It would therefore be more correct to speak of a dislocation or of a kind of "deterritorialisation" of the media (which, even if it saves raw materials, is extremely energy-intensive).[346] What seems to be confirmed by the adoption of digital technologies and dissemination on the web is the centrality of a general rule for the constitution of any musical object: the essential thing, in the end, is (the integrity of) the trace and not the (type of) medium.

This same regulatory principle, however, prompts us to pay particular attention to the production of traces in digital formats, especially where they result from the conversion of traces produced in an analogue environment. For, it should be emphasized, it is indeed the trace – and not only the medium – that changes. It is well known that such a conversion is anything but a neutral operation, especially where the formats adopted are based on the principle – which has become essential on the web – of lossy compression (or bit-rate reduction).[347] It is a problem that has been the subject of much debate because its implications are multiple at the technical, economic and social levels. As Jonathan Sterne observed, "Encoded in every MP3 are whole worlds of possible and impossible sound and whole histories of sonic practices."[348] In fact,

345 To get an idea of their imposing materiality, just take a look at the image of a Google datacentre: https://www.google.com/intl/fr/about/datacenters/.

346 See Kyle, Devine, "L'intensité matérielle de l'écoute musicale sous forme de données," in *Où va la musique? Numérimorphose et nouvelles expériences d'écoute*, ed. Philippe Le Guern (Paris: Presses des Mines, 2016), 58–59.

347 A bit-rate reduction is said to be lossy if after decompression the data differs from the original data. Some of the most common compression formats for audio are AC-3, MP3, Ogg Vorbis, WMA, AU, ASF, AA, AAC – a set in which MP3 still has the lion's share, as observed by Jonathan Sterne, *MP3: The Meaning of a Format. Sign, Storage, Transmission* (Durham: Duke University Press, 2012), 1.

348 Sterne, *MP3: The Meaning of a Format*, 2.

the principle of eliminating redundant data can lead to sound reproduction far from that which might have been envisaged in an analogue environment.

As we have seen, a recording does not necessarily constitute the musical work itself: only works that have been constructed in the studio are concerned,[349] as in most electronic, rock and pop music. Now, the return to these genres – surprisingly enough – to the production of LPs (and devices intended for their reproduction) undoubtedly results partly from the desire to achieve the reality of a more "concrete" object, likely to be collected or offered as a gift, but also from the need to find a sound closer to the one produced in the original trace. One could observe that these are "niche" products, compared to a market that is now generally massively and probably irreversibly oriented towards digital technology; their emergence is nevertheless increasingly significant – in France, mass distribution brands such as FNAC or Cultura now almost all have a vinyl department.

Even if it can be misleading to speak of dematerialisation, we can nevertheless recognize that the migration of music onto digital platforms has had a real impact on its production, having imposed a general conversion of traces into the new formats that have emerged with the web. Let us now attempt to identify this impact in relation to the three modes of operation of musical works discussed throughout this part.

As far as oral works are concerned (and in keeping with the argument we have just made), they may already have had their first great advantage: their ease of access. Let us note it once again: never before has it been possible to travel as much as today to the musical cultures of the whole world – and, of course, in their crossovers and hybridization. At any given moment, one can listen to (and compare, thanks to the large number of examples at our disposal) Irish dances, Armenian melodies, African polyrhythms, etc., as well as to a wide range of other musical styles. Digital recording technologies offer unprecedented possibilities in the implementation and circulation of these heritages. Musicians specializing in different traditions manage to produce original performances, possibly correcting small rhythmic errors or the accuracy of a performance by fine-tuning these aspects in the editing process, where all the parameters of the sound (including its spatiality) are subject to the control of a sound engineer. These productions are generally multimedia

349 In the terms of Roger Pouivet, "La triple ontologie des deux sortes d'enregistrements musicaux," in *Musique et enregistrement*, ed. Pierre-Henry Frangne and Hervé Lacombe (Rennes: Presses Universitaires de Rennes, 2014), 167–170, the ontological model of "constitution" concerns only works based on a constructive type of recording.

and this increasingly so, either combining music with a video, or in the form of a video document.

Where the reception of this type of document is supported by sufficiently developed contextual knowledge, the principle on which oral tradition is based does not seem to be really called into question: if we know the origin of the song "Milia vattu sa Trota,"[350] we will take what we listen to as one of the possible instantiations of the model on which it is based, that of a *canto a tenores*. We will certainly be able to observe that its availability in the media can favour forms of reception that do not take its morphological and performative characteristics sufficiently into account, characteristics that are linked to the possibilities of phonation of the guttural voice, to the phonation specific to the way of singing from one zone to another, to the interplay between soloist and ensemble, etc. Certainly, this constitutes a more general problem that concerns the functioning of any kind of work, the understanding of which requires the mastery of a set of categories and capacities on the part of the listener. On the other hand, it could be assumed that this mode of diffusion will have an impact on the aesthetic functioning of these heritages in the long term. If the recording of an oral work remains in principle the document of a singular performance, its wider diffusion will probably not remain without consequences on the reconfiguration of the artistically salient aspects of the trace to which it refers. To realize this, it suffices to look – as sound studies have done – at the way in which signal processing software or a "beat tracking" algorithm can modify and model the original sound image often without our knowledge, with a decisive impact both on the properties of the object and on our perceptive attitudes.[351]

Let us now turn to works based on a score. As it is the score that is supposed to play the main normative role (and not one of its interpretations, insofar as this can be considered valid or exemplary), it is not surprising therefore to note that the advent of digital interfaces has not brought about any significant changes. Moreover, if in the production of much contemporary music the role of the composer remains institutionally distinct from that of the performer, we have also increasingly seen (since the 1960s) the integration of forms of expression that go beyond the status of music as an art of the trace, by bringing out its second (or first, according to certain scholars) nature as an eminently performative art. The musician's improvisational abilities, and sometimes his

---

350 https://www.youtube.com/watch?v=xSSWrZ_4xb4.

351 See Martin Scherzinger, "Perceptual Modeling in the Era of Music's Automation," unpublished paper, in the Conference of the Società Italiana di Musicologia (Matera: Università della Basilicata, 19 octobre 2019).

corporeality, are readily showcased. In addition, the development of mixed music, based on the combination of acoustic instruments with electronic and digital tools, or on the use of real-time electronics, has also contributed to redefining the scope of the score. Are all these trends – which began to manifest themselves long before the advent of the web – in some way conditioned by the latter? It is still difficult to say, even if we can assume that the increasing importance given to the visual dimension could in the short term further enhance the performative and improvisational capacities of performing musicians. In so far as it has assimilated the new production and distribution technologies, a work based on a score remains anchored to its own normativity.[352]

Let us now turn to the works resulting from a phonographic construction. It is easy to see that digital technology has played a fundamental role in modifying the production criteria for these works, with the dissemination of software and hardware that is economically affordable for an ever-increasing number of users (the home studio, the digital audio station or DAW). In the meantime, streaming sites such as Spotify, Deezer, Soundcloud or Mixcloud have become important distribution channels for professional artists, with a direct consequence in terms of the overall increase in the production of this type of work. Does such production (or, in most cases, self-production) include ontological innovations (and not only economic and social ones)?

Let us first consider the fact that some phonographic works produced by analogue recording systems have generally been converted to digital formats. As we have already remarked, this transformation is not insignificant for any kind of musical recording; it is even less so when considering this kind of work. The loss of data due to compression actually determines a new sound reality. We can add that digital encoding involves operations such as filtering (of noise interference, such as tape hiss), frequency rebalancing, in short all these "remediation" operations that are essential when one wishes to adapt the track to new environments.[353]

All these circumstances may well call into question the ontology of phonographic works. If in order to enhance their "sound image" we need to adapt the trace to the new listening standards linked to digital equipment, these

352 One can only agree with what Vincent Tiffon, "Pour une médiologie musicale comme mode original de connaissance," 131, observed some fifteen years ago: "In short, in the era of electroacoustic music and industrial techno or 'electronic' music [...] supposed to kill the music of the graphosphere, instrumental music in score format is more alive than ever."

353 Angelo Orcalli, "Recorded music: from the ethics of preservation to the critical editing," in *Sounds, Voices and Codes From the Twentieth Century. The Critical Editing of Music at Mirage*, ed. Luca Cossettini and Angelo Orcalli, (Udine: Mirage, 2017), 6.

ultimately prove to be less definitive or "eternal"[354] than one might think. Or we could say that phonographic works turn out to be less "dense" or "saturated" than expected: their "remediation" shows that their density should not be considered as an absolute value. Let us also think of even more significant operations such as remastering (a technique which of course already existed in the analogue environment, but which has developed and spread enormously thanks to digital technology) and, even more clearly, remixing. Remastering will determine a modification of the identifying properties of the original work: in a certain sense, it is an unreliable operation, but one that meets a present need in the context of reception (it is a question of improving the audio standard and adapting it to current, generally higher, requirements). With remixes, the musical universe has ended up being populated by new entities, halfway between sound design techniques and modes of appropriation typical of popular music.

Within the universe of "digital native" works, musical creation has been confronted with new issues. As has rightly been pointed out, one of the most important innovations of the last twenty years has probably been the use of the sampler: an "artefact to the power of 2" which, without producing any sound by itself, can "produce every sound imaginable," thus effectively eliminating the distinction between master and copy.[355] As a reminder, the first device was launched in 1979 and several groups (such as Kraftwerk) used it as early as the 1980s. But it is perhaps above all from the 2000s, with the "democratization" of computer music and CAM, but also with the rise of the DJ and hip-hop, that its use has been extraordinarily successful. Editing, vocoders, sampling, sound shaping, and mash-up are now the order of the day in the pop world. Today, with a sampler (or even with a simple computer, which can perform the same functions), one can create a piece from sound samples of all kinds: acoustic, synthetic or recorded sounds. It is also possible to take and manipulate segments of works from the past. One might say that this brings together what composers have always done: are not the works of Bach, Mozart and Brahms full of quotations and musical references of all kinds? There is, however, a significant difference: the trace that one takes (or imports) is now the sample of an autographic work. In a way, it is as if we were picking up a piece from a Brancusi statue, rather than a Bach melody. Of course, one would say that the sculpture is singular, which is not the case with a record by the Beatles or by Queen. Nevertheless, if you take a chord or a riff from the latter with a

354 This aspect is stressed by Pouivet, *Philosophie du rock*, 63.

355 Philippe Le Guern, "Irreversible. Musique et technologies en régime numérique," *Réseaux* 172 (2012): 45–47.

sampler, what you import is a sample of a work that, in a way, comes directly from the hand of the artist who created it. This runs the risk of muddying the waters as regards the very identity of the works: it is more difficult in principle to determine where the work of one artist begins and ends with another – in other words, what can be identified as an import or plagiarism.[356] We may have entered a phase of global transformation of the very conception of the creative act: *bricolage*, collage and sampling seem to bring back an older, artisanal model to the forefront of artistic invention. Shaken by multiple imports and quotations, the unity of the work (at least as we have defined it) seems to be wavering. As Vincent Tiffon succinctly put it, "it is because the work exists that it can be cited. But by generalizing the citation process, we can go so far as to dissolve the very notion of work."[357]

It should be noted that techniques such as mash-up or xenochrony (developed by Frank Zappa) were introduced long before the digital era. This is quite true, but digital technology has popularized what only a professional studio could do in the past; as for the web, it has allowed the emergence around these techniques of distribution and circulation channels that have made it the heart of new musical genres. Linked to Web 2.0 (the participative and interactive web of social media), productions in genres such as "hauntology" and "chillwave" are characterized by a principle of distributed and participative creativity[358] which, without displaying artistic pretensions – nor renouncing them entirely – puts copyright legislation to the test, weakening the principle of "authorship" by borrowing from known works that are made to function in entirely new and constantly evolving contexts. The figure of the composer/creator thus ends up being called into question (or even sometimes simply abandoned). On the other hand, it must be stressed that in genres based on the import and modification of previous traces, the boundaries between works and improvisations seem decidedly less clear-cut. Is this a temporary phenomenon or a sign of a process of transformation in the way music is created? Or, in other words, is this the symptom of an emerging creative perspective that is increasingly alien to the aesthetics of genius, likely to replace it by a

356 On this topic, see Frédéric Döhl, *Mashup in der Musik. Fremdreferenzielles Komponieren, Sound Sampling und Urheberrecht* (Blelefeld: Transcript, 2016); Alessandro Bertinetto, Ezio Gamba and Davide Sisto, "Introduzione," *Estetica. Studi e ricerche* (Special issue: "Ladri di musica. Filosofia, musica e plagio") 1 (2014), 5–12.

357 Vincent Tiffon, "La partition, le phonographe et l'échantillonneur: usages de la copie en musique, " *Déméter* (2003), 6.

358 See Georgina Born and Christopher Haworth, "From Microsound To Vaporwave: Internet-Mediated Musics, Online methods, and Genre," *Music & Letters* 98/4 (2017), 11.

poetics of borrowing, appropriation, exchange and negotiation?[359] The evolution over the next twenty years will probably provide us with the beginnings of an answer. For the moment, we can see that, despite their omnipresence on the web, these productions are not comparable – judging by the (very simple) criterion of the number of viewings – to the more traditional productions focused on the making of an original "hit," of medium length and easily attributable to a singer or an author.

At the same time, it seems unlikely that the status of "the work" can actually disintegrate into a creative model that would relegate music, so to speak, to the status of collective or improvised art. On the one hand, it can be observed that in all musical genres, the economic and cultural apparatus of Western capitalist societies persists in revolving around the idea of creation linked to a clearly identifiable artistic individuality. The fundamental reason for this may not even be economic, but rather anthropological: inasmuch as the idea of objectifying and individualizing an artistic act has formed slowly over the course of history, it appears as one of the many possible variations of the idea, linked to one of our deepest human needs, of leaving a lasting imprint.

Let us take a closer look at a few aspects concerning the morphology of these kinds of works produced on digital platforms. In the context of pop, if albums continue to be produced, the production of singles with a "canonical" length of 3–4 minutes (i.e., roughly the same duration as in the 45 rpm disc era) seems to be gradually gaining ground. The principle of "mesoscopy"[360] is to some extent largely confirmed. A recent study based on the theory of attentional economics[361] tells us more about their morphological characteristics. In the most popular songs, there is a tendency to eliminate or considerably reduce the instrumental introduction (from 20 seconds to a maximum of 5 seconds – but more generally to 0 seconds – often occupied by four repetitions of the first bar, the trademark of Pharell Williams). Other trends are: to condense the title into a single word; to present the chorus very quickly (no more than 30 seconds); to use the chorus-couplet-chorus pattern; to eliminate instrumental solos; to produce a compressed and synthetic sound (with dynamics based on a mix that favours MP3 listening on speakers or cheap headphones). In short, everything seems to be done to favour easy identification and to hold the listener's attention. The song changes according to the new medium: its

359 Bertinetto, Gamba and Sisto, "Introduzione," 7.

360 See above, part 2, 58.

361 Hubert Léveillé Gauvin, "Drawing listener attention in popular music: Testing five musical features arising from the theory of attention economy," *Musicae Scientiae* 22/3 (2018): 291–304.

morphology is closer to the sort of music one hears in ads (i.e. more incisive and focused). It is as if the biggest danger were to skip tracks (a danger that becomes very real if the sound or the chorus does not satisfy).

Other trends include the association of musical traces with visual traces (which has become almost systematic since the advent of Web 2.0). Several main ways of combining sound and image are emerging. These include: the (simple) representation of the cover or sleeve of the original production, which recalls a "more or less explicit remediation of the culture of the record";[362] the representation of the face and name of the singer or musician staged, as "marks of individuality," based on television and radio models; and new creations based on "the combinatorial and playful dimension permitted by audiovisual publishing software."[363] The importance recently assumed by the latter option is perhaps a sign that musical works – particularly of the phonographic kind – now tend to be incorporated into multimedia works.[364] The visualization of electronic music has experimented with several solutions, ranging from the most abstract, such as the creation of what have been called "synesthetic datascapes," to combining images of more concrete objects that are subject to an "analytical vision," to finally adopting the aesthetics of video-games.[365] These are often original artistic productions, which demand to be considered in all their expressive uniqueness,[366] even if sometimes the musicians may also return to the idea of a filmed performance. We can see in this a new symptom of the weakening of the model of the musical work as an autonomous sound structure in favour of an increasingly hybrid product, based on an interartistic and multimedia convergence that requires an updating of our sensitive and cognitive capacities in order to be appreciated and understood.

The emergence of the multimedia dimension leads us to examine another original invention specific to the Web 2.0 era: the "app album" or the "disco-app." The origin of this invention can be traced back to the National Mall

362 Heuguet, Guillaume (2016). "YouTube, la musique et moi," in *Où va la musique? Numérimorphose et nouvelles expériences d'écoute*, ed. Philippe Le Guern (Paris: Presses des Mines, 2016), 148.

363 Heuguet, "YouTube, la musique et moi," 149.

364 See Carol Vernallis, *Unruly Media: YouTube, Music Video, and the New Digital Cinema* (New York: Oxford University Press, 2013).

365 Allan Cameron, "Instrumental Visions. Electronica, Music Video and the Environmental Interface," in *The Oxford Handbook of Sound and Image in Digital Media*, ed. Carol Vernallis, Amy Herzog, and John Richardson (Oxford, Oxford University Press, 2013), 757–764.

366 As stressed by Antoine Gaudin, "Le vidéoclip, un art populaire intermédial à l'ère numérique: enjeux épistémologiques." In: *Le levain des médias. Forme, format, média*, ed. Guillaume Soulez G. and Kira Kitsopanidou (Paris: L'Harmattan, 2015), 167–177.

project (2011) by the American duo Bluebrain: an app in which the tracks changed according to the listener's geolocation on the National Mall in Washington D.C. This first example was followed by *Biophilia*, by the Icelandic singer Björk.[367] Other artists have subsequently exploited such possibilities, such as Massive Attack (with Fantom), Peter Gabriel (Music Tiles), and Radiohead (PolyFauna). These albums are built on the model of the playlist and video games, designed in a way to suit the listener-receiver's sensitivity and initiative. Would this procedure signal the end of the concept-album? To temper this impression, one might notice that these phenomena remain relatively minor for the moment. If the ideal, in terms of production, has become the conception of a single, the hit capable of totalizing the greatest number of views,[368] rock bands and many artists also continue to produce more traditional albums (generally burned on CD and, in limited edition, on vinyl), which blogs and reference magazines (such as the historical "Rolling Stone" or the French "Les Inrockuptibles") continue to report regularly. However, the way they are presented and offered to the public on social media leads us to believe that the path opened by app-albums is revealing. In fact, the work – which in this case coincides with the recording artefact – is thought out from the outset in a more open and interactive way, by imagining new strategies likely to give the listener more initiative. In this sense, it is conceived as a complex media object, addressing new, faster and more concentrated attentional mechanisms, based on new perceptive behaviours.

This consideration prompts us to return once again to some of the consequences that have been associated with the production of phonographic works, in particular the conditions which seem to bring them closer, in certain musical genres, to the products of popular culture. On the one hand, what is being produced and broadcast today on streaming music platforms is largely consistent with that mode of production, given that it was designed for its wider distribution. However, in other respects, current production seems to run counter to the idea of a mass art form. Behind the wide accessibility of popular culture, there was an aim to manipulate, control or direct taste and society from above. In other words, this art was conceived in a vertical relationship between professional agents linked to related industries (and of course to economic power) on the one hand and (presumed) undifferentiated and passive consumers on the other. It is legitimate to ask whether such a relationship still exists in the world of social media. There is certainly the impression

367 For an interesting commentary of this work see Ghosn, *Musiques numériques*, 29–34.

368 At the top of YouTube's hit parade is "Despacito" (Louis Fonsi ft. Daddy Yankee) with, as of 17 May 2020, over 6.76 billion views (the total in under three years).

that our tastes are being guided by the big data companies. Google, Facebook and Amazon have been in our homes for a long time now and, thanks to recommendations based on the use of increasingly precise and personalized algorithms, offer us choices that can follow, but also "shape" and sometimes "homologate" (if we want to use a Pasolinian term) our preferences according to economic interests.[369] But the assumption of control from above also seems to lose its coherence because of this same system, which has probably left much more initiative to the auditor/spectator, in an information flow where it is difficult to understand the cause and effect of a certain change in attention mechanisms. In what has been called the "algorithmic culture,"[370] a greater individualization of aesthetic consumption seems to be the counterpart of the outsourcing and automation of information search and selection processes.[371] While it increases the social dimension of many musical genres, the Internet allows everyone to access a kind of large universal music library where they can not only find their happiness but also leave their mark. It has thus ended up encouraging the formation of new cognitive capacities which are more flexible and mobile modes of listening that generally differ from the LP era (one need only think of the importance taken by a phenomenon such as the compilation of playlists).[372]

As we have already pointed out, the development of self-production has to be understood at the same time as the modification of the norms of listening, in a situation that has given rise to new conceptual conflicts about the identity of works. We are led to admit that a vertical relationship, such as that established by media such as radio or television, no longer has the meaning it once had: the production of works seems to respond to an increasingly differentiated demand from consumers – who have also become important producers of information. Algorithm-based recommendation systems can certainly be oriented to provoke, if not a "formatting" of tastes, at least forms of frictionless experiences, "fundamentally at odds with aesthetic experience."[373] But this

369 See Lucien Perticoz, "Opulence musicale et recommandation. Quelques réserves fa e à une 'révolution' en cours," in *Où va la musique? Numérimorphose et nouvelles expériences d'écoute*, ed. Philippe Le Guern (Paris: Presses des Mines, 2016), 127–140.

370 Ted Striphas, "Algorithmic culture," *European Journal of Cultural* Studies 18 (2015), 395–412.

371 Emanuele Arielli, "Taste and the algorithm," *Studi di estetica*, 46/3 (2018), 78.

372 See Esteban Buch, "On the Evolution of Private Record Collections: a Short Story," in *Musical Listening in the Age of Technological Reproduction*, ed. Gianmario Borio (Farnham: Ashgate, 2015), 41–52 and Anja Nylund Hagen, "The Playlist Experience: Personal Playlists in Music Streaming Services," *Popular Music and Society*, March (2015), 1–19.

373 Nancy Weiss Hanrahan, "La découverte musicale en régime numérique." in *Où va la musique? Numérimorphose et nouvelles expériences d'écoute*, ed. Philippe Le Guern (Paris: Presses des Mines, 2016), 78.

phenomenon is perhaps counterbalanced by opposing phenomena. We are witnessing the emergence of companies whose aim is to improve the tools of discovery and to explore new ways of recommendation.[374] More generally, we can also think of the formation of autonomous micro-cultures or subcultures (what Jean Molino called the phenomenon of cultural "tribalization"[375] fifteen years ago). Think of the vast universe of hip hop, dubstep, reggaeton, afrobeats, and even chillwave or vaporwave: these are all commercial genres, but one would be somewhat hesitant to classify them under the term of mass art.

When we first listen to it, a vaporwave production can indeed appear as a repetitive, captivating background sound, a kind of elevator or waiting room music. Is it possible to base a worldwide hit on such characteristics? In spite of appearances, artists do not stop being original in the way they sequence the background sound, use retro stereophonic or compression effects and forms of sound degradation that immerse us in the soundscapes of the 80s, in sync with almost motionless images, dominated by the artificiality of neon light. Compared to any worldwide hit, a work of this type is nevertheless a niche product (which is confirmed, among other things, by the smaller number of views), aimed at an audience of afficionados who have formed their own taste through watching videos and familiarity with the procedures of digital manipulation of sound and image, in an exchange of information expressed in often quite technical language. Fixed in an audio-visual trace that remains easily accessible via streaming sites, such a work looks like an artefact whose aesthetic properties cannot, in our opinion, be grasped by an undifferentiated and unprepared public.

To sum up, the advent of digital platforms and the web has had a strong impact on phonographic works – much more prominent, in any case, than it may have had on score-based and oral works. This is not surprising, considering that phonography has been at the origin of the most important ontological discontinuities in the musical world over the last 150 years. In addition to bringing out the social nature of these works in an unprecedented way, digital platforms have fostered important transformations in their morphology as well as in their operating modes. The expansion of remastering and remixing techniques has called into question the principle of their ontological saturation,

374 Cédric Claquin and Pierre-René Lhérisson, "Explorer de nouvelles expériences de recommandation et d'usages," in *Où va la musique? Numérimorphose et nouvelles expériences d'écoute*, ed. Philippe Le Guern (Paris: Presses des Mines, 2016), 153–165.

375 Jean Molino, "Technologie, mondialisation tribalisation. Un survol rétrospectif du XXe siècle," in *Musiques: une encyclopédie pour le XXIe siècle. 1. Musiques du XXe siècle*, ed. Jean-Jaques Nattiez (Arles and Paris: Actes Sud et Cité de la musique, 2003), 69–86.

whereas sampling and mash-up has done the same for the principle of authorship that had accompanied them in the radio and television era. By addressing more inattentive and short-lived forms of reception, they look like artefact-recordings designed in a more open, interactive or modular way, able to incorporate an explicitly multimedia dimension.

Conclusions

The time has come to take stock of where we are. After having developed a discussion on the ambivalence of musical art and the meaning of some of its main concepts, we have advocated a conception of musical works that defines them as sound artefacts belonging more generally to the category of "social objects." We have stressed that their functioning is aesthetic and their nature social – which means admitting that their existence depends on the fixing of a trace. For this to be correctly recognized and identified, the presence of some specific categories and capacities is indispensable. An inscriptionist and contextualist principle governs this relationship: a musical work is not understood purely as a sound structure, but as a structure rich in properties that integrate artistic intentionality and that assumes extensive normative value depending on its contexts of production and reception.

Insofar as the existence of the musical works depends on such an inscription, in order to understand how they function, it was important to draw attention to how such traces are fixed and what these traces refer to, and in particular to distinguish three main options: orality, notation and phonography. We have observed the extent to which these three technological paradigms and the normativity that accompanies them differ. Considering the work in the light of this tripartition allows us to make a first general identification of the way it functions aesthetically. In the case of orality, the possibilities of varying or adapting what is prescribed by a performance considered as a model are important; stricter rules govern the performances of score-based music and another normativity concerns phonographic works, whose ontological density cannot be considered as an absolute value. Thus, a cover version of an Abba song will be distinguished from the interpretation of a Schubert *Lied* on the basis of an ontological difference: fundamentally, the one that exists between the ontological density of a phonographic work (which can give rise to covers or performances that meet the principles of orality) and the allographic functioning of a score-based work (that governs an interpretation based on the principle of the *Werktreue*).

A study of the ways in which traces are fixed – even or perhaps precisely where they may appear complex, precarious or ambiguous – is in our view necessary for building up our knowledge of musical works and for forming a correct judgement of them. However, as we have stressed, this exercise should take into account the fundamental ambivalence of the musical art we spoke of in the first part: an art situated in the field of forces between trace and performativity. Distinguishing and implementing the right categories allows us to understand the true nature of the musical object we are studying and to understand its specific normativity. Thus, when we listen to an electroacoustic work or to a rock album, we are less inclined to focus on a type in the sounds we are hearing than to accept them as they are (re-)presented to us by the recording. On the other hand, if we listen to a work that has come down to us via an oral tradition, the action of the musician will be considered as a model of a trace or an outline present in the memory of a given community. Basically, having the right categories is necessary in order to identify the right artefact and to have the right experience of it.

While it may seem uncomfortable or somewhat artificial to underline the existence of different functioning in what, in everyday language, may appear to be one and the same work, it can be observed that this distinction only highlights what is already implicit in our relationship to different musical artefacts. In other words, we would stress that this is not only a speculative issue: musicians, music critics and musicologists are constantly confronted with this kind of problem. Interpreting, listening to or judging the performance of a Bob Dylan song is not like playing, listening to or judging the performance of a standard from the Real Book or a *rebetiko*: in each of these cases, the originality, beauty and coherence of what the musician does and what the listener says will depend in part on a prior understanding of the object in relation to the contexts and forms of life that accompanied its production and its reception. It is the implementation of this preliminary understanding that we wanted to focus on in this essay.

The reader might have the impression that we have mainly focused on oral and phonographic works, treating score-based works in a cursory way. This is probably true, and the latter would have deserved a more in-depth study; at the same time, it is a debate in which our knowledge seems to be more solid, since the scholarly community, both musicological and philosophical, has already taken a great interest in it. We cannot say the same of the other two categories: as we have tried to show, the class of phonographic works is very rich and, if we exclude rock music, still relatively unexplored; as for the world of orality, it has generally been studied without resorting to the category of work: we hope we have shown why such a category is appropriate, provided that we take into consideration the specific normativity it displays in these contexts.

The tripartition we have developed provides us with a framework for a basic understanding of how musical works function today. However, we should not misunderstand its meaning. It is not a question of imposing a normative framework on reality, but rather of observing whether and how the contexts of production and reception of a musical artefact show that it belongs to a certain way of fixing and transmitting the trace, and how a musical culture is mainly organized. It goes without saying that some cases will only partially fit into one or the other of these categories. It would not be a question, in this case, of trying to "force" them into a Procrustean bed: their interest often lies precisely in their capacity to oscillate between one category and the other – or, if we prefer, to manifest a certain ontological ambiguity. Let us take as a last example of such an ambiguity "You Don't Know What Love Is" (by Don Raye and Gene DePaul), the jazz standard from the Real Book that we mentioned in the first part. Such a piece normally has a title, a text, and an author; yet it would be inappropriate to conceive of it as a score-based work. The reason is that when we consider the most common ways of performing it, we can see that it functions as the starting point of an improvisational path that refers to its general morphology but at the same time lends itself to be appreciated for its own qualities. Thus, a piano and voice rendition that complies perfectly with what is notated in the score of the *Real Book* would be certainly regarded as a poor or sketchy version of the piece. Here the degree of improvisation and arrangement of what is played can obviously vary – and it is surely one of the most interesting aspects of this type of performance; but in principle, it cannot be equal to zero. And yet, it is true that sometimes a jazz standard can be presented in a version that is closer to its (simple) melodic-harmonic structure:[376] in this case, it could be said that it functions as a "thin" musical work, or one situated midway between an orally-transmitted work (capable of being arranged, orchestrated and varied to some extent) and a notated work.

The idea that the different ways of functioning of musical works can coexist, and that a work of a certain type can give rise to performative acts that seem to refer to another type of work (and to another normativity), might in some respects give the impression of dragging the argument into a kind of relativism that ends up liquidating the idea of an ontological identity. However, we believe that this impression can be tempered by studying the effective functioning of each artefact in the contexts of its production and reception. Indeed, for each of them, the principle of the prevalence of an identification

376 This dual possibility of conceiving jazz standards has been thematized by Davies, *Musical Works and Performances*, 16–19. See above §1.5.

criterion applies: if we listen to a rock band in concert, what we expect to hear are not the properties of their phonographic work they have produced in the studio but a performance that, taking the latter as a model, assumes the guise of an oral work. Even if it turns out to be dependent on the studio version, and even if it manifests this dependence by a morphological similarity that is audibly detectable, the latter functions by following its own normativity. The authenticity that we ask for in the cover version differs fundamentally from the authenticity we ask of the recording artefact, albeit possibly remastered for broadcast on digital platforms.

This solution certainly has the disadvantage of multiplying the categories (and the corresponding entities); I hope this inconvenience is however compensated by better understanding how the musical works function in our actual experience. It seems more correct to say that what in principle looks like a single song actually coincides with several artefacts that obey different rules, rather than making it coincide with a single sound structure that we would be forced to consider as fundamentally abstract or ideal. To approach the question in a different way, it would be a mistake to think that understanding the work can be abstracted from the way it is presented or enacted: if we highlight what happens in the most common listening situations, we realize that we are dealing with very different categories, objects and attentional capacities. In any case, I hope that the arguments I have presented in this essay have contributed to clarifying such a network of concepts and objects, shedding light on a meaningful portion of the rich musical reality in which we are immersed.

Acknowledgements

I would like to express my sincere thanks to Tiziana Andina, who first suggested that I write this essay and who had the patience to wait so long for the manuscript. I owe a special thanks to Alessandro Bertinetto, Richard Hermann, Jerrold Levinson and Nicolò Palazzetti, whose remarks and comments have been very useful in clarifying ideas and improving the text. Many thanks also to Jean-Yves Bart, from the translation and editing department of the "Maison des Sciences de l'Homme d'Alsace" (MISHA), who translated the introduction and the first part, and to Philip Clarke, who revised the translation of the full text. Finally, for the financial support provided for this revision, my gratitude goes to the "Groupe de Recherches Expérimentales sur l'Acte Musical" (Labex GREAM) at the University of Strasbourg, as part of the "Programme d'Investissement d'Avenir (PIA)" ANR-10-LBX-27 and to the interdisciplinary institute that has succeeded it, the "Centre de Recherche et d'Expérimentation sur l'Acte Artistique" (CREAA).

Bibliography

Adorno, Theodor Wiesengrund. *Aesthetic Theory*. Edited by Gretel Adorno and Rolf Tiedemann. Translated by Robert Hullot-Kentor. London – New York: Continuum, 2002.

Adorno, Theodor Wiesengrund. *Mahler. A Musical Physiognomy*. Translated by Edmund Jephcott. Chicago and London: University of Chicago Press, 1996.

Adorno, Theodor Wiesengrund. "On the Fetish-Character in Music and the Regression of Listening." In *Essays on Music*, edited by Richard Leppert, translated by Susan Gillespie, 288–317. Berkeley & Los Angeles: University of California Press, 2002.

Alperson, Philippe. "On Musical Improvisation." *Journal of Aesthetics and Art Criticism* 43, no. 1 (1984): 17–29.

Andina, Tiziana. *What is Art? The Question of Definition Reloaded*. Leiden: Brill, 2017.

Arbo, Alessandro. *Il suono instabile. Saggi sulla filosofia della musica nel Novecento*. Torino: Trauben, 2000.

Arbo, Alessandro. "Jugement esthétique et ontologie musicale." *International Review of Aesthetics and Sociology of Music* 45, 1 (2014): 3–19.

Arielli, Emanuele. "Taste and the algorithm." *Studi di estetica* 46, 3 (2018): 77–97.

Arom, Simha. "Réalisations, variations, modèles dans les musiques traditionnelles centrafricaines." In *L'improvisation dans les musiques de tradition orale*, edited by Bernard Lortat Jacob, 119–122. Paris: Selaf, 1987.

Assante, Ernesto. *Copio, dunque sono. La rivoluzione elettronica che ha cambiato la musica*. Roma: Coniglio Editore, 2009.

Austin, John L. *How to Do Things with Words*. Oxford: Oxford University Press, 1962.

Baroni, Mario, Rossana Dalmonte and Carlo Jacoboni. *Le regole della musica. Indagine sui meccanismi della comunicazione*. Torino: EDT, 1999.

Barrett, James. "Producing Performance." In *Recorded Music. Performance, Culture and Technology*, edited by Amanda Bayley, 89–106. Cambridge: Cambridge University Press, 2010.

Bartel, Christopher. "Music without Metaphysics." *British Journal of Aesthetics* 51 (2011), 383–98.

Benjamin, Walter. *The Work of Art in the Age of Its Technological Reproducibility and Other Writings on Media*. Edited by Michael W. Jennings, Brigid Doherty & Thomas Y. Levin. Translated by Edmund Jephcott, Rodney Livingstone, Howard Eiland & others. Cambridge, Mass. & London: Harvard University Press, 2008.

Bertinetto, Alessandro. "Paganini Does Not Repeat. Improvisation And The Type/Token Ontology," *Teorema* XXXI/3 (2012), 105–126.

Bertinetto, Alessandro. "4 minuti e 33 secondi di arte. Non di musica." In *John Cage. Una rivoluzione lunga cent'anni*. Edited by Giacomo Fronzi, 155–175. Milano: Mimesis, 2012.

Bertinetto, Alessandro. *Eseguire l'inatteso. Ontologia della musica e improvvisazione*. Roma: Il glifo, 2016.

Bertinetto, Alessandro. "Improvisation and Ontology of Art." *Rivista di Estetica* 73 (2020), 10–29.

Bertinetto, Alessandro, Gamba, Ezio and Sisto, Davide. "Introduzione." *Estetica. Studi e ricerche* (Special issue: *Ladri di musica. Filosofia, musica e plagio*, edited by Alessandro Bertinetto, Ezio Gamba and Davide Sisto) 1 (2014): 5–12.

Born, Georgina and Haworth, Christopher. "From Microsound To Vaporwave: Internet-Mediated Musics, Online methods, and Genre." *Music & Letters* 98, 4 (2017): 1–47.

Brown, Lee B. "Musical Works, Improvisation, and the Principle of Continuity." *Journal of Aesthetics and Art Criticism* 54 (1996): 353–369.

Brown, Lee B. "Phonography, Rock Records, and the Ontology of Recorded Music." *The Journal of Aesthetics and Art Criticism* 58, No. 2 (2000): 361–372.

Brown, Lee B., "Improvisation." In *The Routledge Companion of Philosophy and Music*, edited by Theodore Gracyk and Andrew Kania, 59–69. London and New York: Routledge, 2011.

Brunello, Mario and Zagrebelsky, Gustavo. *Interpretare. Dialogo tra un musicista e un giurista*. Bologna: Il Mulino, 2016.

Buch, Esteban. "On the Evolution of Private Record Collections: a Short Story." In *Musical Listening in the Age of Technological Reproduction*, edited by Gianmario Borio, 41–52. Farnham: Ashgate, 2015.

Cameron, Allan. "Instrumental Visions. Electronica, Music Video and the Environmental Interface." In *The Oxford Handbook of Sound and Image in Digital Media*, edited by Carol Vernallis, Amy Herzog, and John Richardson, 752–772. Oxford: Oxford University Press, 2013.

Cameron, Ross P. "There Are No Things That Are Musical Works." *British Journal of Aesthetics* 48, n. 3 (2008): 295–314.

Canonne, Clément. "Sur l'ontologie de l'improvisation." In *Ontologie musicale: perspectives et débats*, edited by Alessandro Arbo and Marcello Ruta, 279–320. Paris: Hermann, 2014.

Canonne, Clément. "L'appréciation esthétique de l'improvisation." *Aisthesis* 6, n. 3 (2014): 331–356. https://oajournals.fupress.net/index.php/aisthesis/article/view/826.

Caplan, Ben and Matheson, Carl. "Defending Musical Perdurantism." *British Journal of Aesthetics* 46 (2006): 59–69.

Caporaletti, Vincenzo. *I processi improvvisativi nella musica. Un approccio globale*. Lucca: LIM, 2005.

Carpenter, Patricia. "The Musical Object." *Current Musicology* 5 (1967): 56–87.

Carroll, Noël. *Philosophy of Mass Art*. Oxford: Clarendon, 1998.

Chion, Michel. *Guide des objets sonores. Pierre Schaeffer et la recherche musicale*. Paris: Éditions Buchet-Chastel and INA – GRM, 1983.

Claquin, Cédric and Lhérisson, Pierre-René. "Explorer de nouvelles expériences de recommandation et d'usages." In *Où va la musique? Numérimorphose et nouvelles expériences d'écoute*, edited by Philippe Le Guern, 153–165. Paris: Presses des Mines, 2016.

Clarke, Eric. "Understanding the psychology of performance." In *Musical Performance. A Guide to Understanding*, edited by John Rink, 59–72. Cambridge: Cambridge University Press, 2002.

Cook, Nicholas. *Music: A Very Short Introduction*. Oxford: Oxford University Press, 2000.

Cook, Nicholas. "Betweeen Process and Product: Music and/as Performance." *Music Theory Online* 7, n. 2 (2001) http://www.mtosmt.org/issues/mto.01.7.2/mto.01.7.2.cook.html.

Cook, Nicholas. *Beyond the Score: Music as Performance*. Oxford: Oxford University Press, 2013.

Cugny, Laurent. *Analyser le jazz. Analyse du jazz, analyse de l'œuvre*. Paris: Outre Mesure, 2009.

Dahlhaus, Carl. *Esthetics of Music*. Translated by William W. Austin. Cambridge: Cambridge University Press, 1982.

Dalhaus, Carl. *Foundations of Music History*. Translated by J. B. Robinson. Cambridge and London: Cambridge University Press, 1983.

D'Angelo, Paolo. "La definizione dell'arte." In *Introduzione all'estetica analitica*, edited by Paolo D'Angelo, 3–36. Roma – Bari: Laterza, 2008.

Danto, Arthur. "The Artworld." *The Journal of Philosophy* 61/19 (1964): 571–584.

Darsel, Sandrine. "Qu'est-ce qu'une œuvre musicale?" *Klesis. Revue philosophique* 13 (2009): 147–185.

Darsel, Sandrine. *De la musique aux émotions. Une exploration philosophique*. Rennes: Presses Universitaires de Rennes, 2010.

Darsel, Sandrine, "Musique et enregistrement. Une exploration goodmanienne des musiques du monde." In *Ontologie musicale: perspectives et débats*, edited by Alessandro Arbo and Marcello Ruta, 185–203. Paris: Hermann, 2014.

Davies, David. *Art as Performance*. Oxford: Blackwell, 2004.

Davies, David. *Philosophy of the Performing Arts*. Chichester (West Sussex): Wiley – Blackwell, 2011.

Davies, Stephen. *Musical Works and Performances: a Philosophical Exploration*. Oxford: Oxford University Press, 2001.

Davies, Stephen. *Themes in the Philosophy of Music*. Oxford: Oxford University Press, 2003.

Davies, Stephen. "Notations." In *The Routledge Companion to Philosophy and Music*, edited by Theodore Gracyk and Andrew Kania, 70–79. London and New York: Routledge, 2011.

Davies, Stephen. "Works of Music: Approaches to the Ontology of Music from Analytic Philosophy." *Music Research Annual* 1: 1–19. URL: https://musicresearchannual.org/wp-content/uploads/2020/11/daviese28094works-of-music.pdf.

Debruyne, François. "Environnements numériques de l'écoute et culture publique. Vers de nouvelles formes de domestication de l'expérience musicale?" In *Où va la musique? Numérimorphose et nouvelles expériences d'écoute*, edited by Philippe Le Guern, 81–91. Paris: Presses des Mines, 2016.

Delalande, François. "La gestique de Gould: éléments pour une sémiologie du geste musical." In *Glenn Gould Pluriel*, edited by Ghyslaine Guertin, 85–111. Verdun: Louise Courteau, 1988.

Delalande, François. *Le son des musiques. Entre technologie et esthétique*. Paris: INA and Buchet-Chastel, 2001.

Delalande, François. "Le paradigme électroacoustique." In *Musiques: une encyclopédie pour le XXI*e *siècle. Vol. 1 Musiques du XX*e *siècle*, edited by Jean-Jacques Nattiez, 213–233. Arles and Paris: Actes Sud and Cité de la musique, 2003.

Derrida, Jacques. *Psyché. Inventions de l'autre* (t. 1). Paris: Galilée, 1987.

Derrida, Jacques. *Of Grammatology*. Translated by Gayatri Chakravorty Spivak. Baltimore and London: The John Hopkins University Press, 1997.

De Vecchi, Francesca. "Ontologia sociale e intenzionalità: quattro tesi." *Rivista di estetica* 49 (2012): 183–201.

De Vecchi, Francesca. "'Platonismo sociale?' In difesa del realismo fenomenologico in ontologia sociale." *Rivista di estetica* 50 (2012): 75–90.

Devine, Kyle. "L'intensité matérielle de l'écoute musicale sous forme de données." In *Où va la musique? Numérimorphose et nouvelles expériences d'écoute*, edited by Philippe Le Guern, 47–64. Paris: Presses des Mines, 2016.

Dickie, George. "The Myth of the Aesthetic Attitude." *American Philosophical Quarterly* 1, No. 1 (January 1964): 56–65.

Dickie, George. *Art and Aesthetic: An Institutional Analysis*. Ithaca (New York): Cornell University Press, 1974.

Dodd, Julian. *Works of Music: An Essay in Ontology*. Oxford: Oxford University Press, 2007.

Dodd, Julian. "Upholding Standards: A Realist Ontology of Standard Form Jazz," *The Journal of Aesthetics and Art Criticism* 72, n. 3 (2014): 277–290.

Döhl, Frédéric. "Per un campo di dibattito interdisciplinare. A proposito del ruolo dell'esperienza estetica nella giurisprudenza riguardante il copyright." *Estetica.*

Studi e ricerche (Special issue: "Ladri di musica. Filosofia, musica e plagio", edited by Alessandro Bertinetto, Ezio Gamba and Davide Sisto) 1 (2014): 47–58.

Döhl, Frédéric. *Mashup in der Musik. Fremdreferenzielles Komponieren, Sound Sampling und Urheberrecht*. Blelefeld: Transcript, 2016.

During, Jean. *Musiques d'Iran: la tradition en question*. Paris: Geuthner, 2010.

Eco, Umberto. *The Open Work*. Translated by Anna Cancogni. Cambridge, Massachusetts: Harvard University Press, 1989.

Eisenberg, Evan. *The Recording Angel: Music, Records and Culture from Aristotle to Zappa*. New Haven and London: Yale University Press, 2005.

Emmerson, Simon. "In what form can 'live electronic music' live on?" *Organised Sound* 11, n.3 (2006): 209–219.

Fabbri, Franco. *L'ascolto tabù. Le musiche nello scontro globale*. Milano: il Saggiatore, 2017.

Ferraris, Maurizio. *La fidanzata automatica*. Milano: Bombiani, 2007.

Ferraris, Maurizio. *Documentalità. Perché è necessario lasciar tracce*. Roma–Bari: Laterza, 2009.

Ferraris, Maurizio. *Mobilitazione totale*. Roma and Bari: Laterza, 2015.

Frith, Simon. "L'industrialisation de la musique et le problème de la valeur." In *Musiques: une encyclopédie pour le XXIe siècle. Vol. 1 Musiques du XXe siècle*, edited by Jean-Jacques Nattiez, 1132–1146. Arles and Paris: Actes Sud and Cité de la musique, 2003.

Garda, Michela. "Le teorie dell'opera d'arte musicale nel Novecento." In *Storia dei concetti musicali. Espressione, forma, opera*, edited by Gianmario Borio and Carlo Gentili, 295–316. Roma: Carocci, 2007.

Gasparini, Stéphane. "Le *Köln Concert* de Tomasz Trzcinski." In *Quand l'enregistrement change la musique*, edited by Alessandro Arbo and Pierre-Emmanuel Lephay, 219–239. Paris: Hermann, 2017.

Gaudin, Antoine. "Le vidéoclip, un art populaire intermédial à l'ère numérique: enjeux épistémologiques." In *Le levain des médias. Forme, format, média*, edited by Guillaume Soulez and Kira Kitsopanidou, 167–177. Paris: L'Harmattan, 2015.

Genette, Gérard. *L'Œuvre de l'art. 1: immanence et transcendance*. Paris: Seuil, 1994.

Ghirardini, Cristina. "La 'naturale acuta sensibilità all'armonia, al numero ed al metro'. L'improvvisazione poetica in ottava rima in Italia centrale dal Settecento alla prima metà del Novecento." *Fonti musicali italiane* 22 (2017): 55–89.

Ghosn, Joseph. *Musiques numériques. Essai sur la vie nomade de la musique*. Paris: Seuil, 2013.

Giombini, Lisa. *Musical Ontology. A Guide for the Perplexed*. Milano: Mimesis, 2017.

Giuliani, Elizabeth. "Comment l'enregistrement s'effaça devant la musique." In *Musique et enregistrement*, ed. Pierre-Henry Frangne and Hervé Lacombe, 77–94. Rennes: Presses Universitaires de Rennes, 2014.

Godlovitch, Stan. *Musical Performance. A Philosophical Study*, London and New York: Routledge, 1998.

Goehr, Lydia. *The Imaginary Museum of Musical Works. An Essay in the Philosophy of Music*. Oxford: Oxford University Press, 1992.

Goldoni, Daniele. "Composizione e improvvisazione: dove sta la differenza?" *Aisthesis* (special issue: *Ontologie musicali* edited by Alessandro Arbo and Alessandro Bertinetto) 6, n. 3 (2013): 133–153. https://oajournals.fupress.net/index.php/aisthesis/article/view/816.

Goodman, Nelson. *Languages of Art. An Approach to a Theory of Symbols*. Indianapolis: The Bobbs-Merrill Company, 1968.

Goodman, Nelson. *Ways of Worldmaking*. Hassocks: The Harvester Press, 1978.

Goodman, Nelson. "L'art en action," *Les Cahiers du Musée National d'Art Moderne*, 41 (1992): 7–13.

Gould, Glenn. "The Prospects of Recording." In *The Glenn Gould Reader*, edited by Tim Page, 331–353. New York: Alfred A. Knopf, 1989.

Gracyk, Theodore, *Rhythm and Noise: An Aesthetics of Rock*. Durham: Duke University Press, 1996.

Grandjon, Fabien and Combes, Clément. "Digitamorphosis of Music Consumption Practices: The Case of Young Music Lovers." *French Cultural Studies* 20, n. 3 (2009): 287–314.

Guesdom, Maël. "L'ontologie du rock de Roger Pouivet." *Volume. La revue des musiques populaires/The French journal of popular music studies* 7, n. 1 (2010), https://doi.org/10.4000/volume.1094.

Hagen, Anja Nylund. "The Playlist Experience: Personal Playlists in Music Streaming Services." *Popular Music and Society* (March 2015): 1–19.

Hains, Jacques. "Du Ruleau de cire au disque compact." In *Musiques. Une encyclopédie pour le XXI*[e] *siècle. 1. Musiques du XX*[e] *siècle*, edited by Jean-Jacques Nattiez, 901–938. Arles and Paris: Actes Sud and Cité de la musique, 2003.

Hamilton, Andy. *Aesthetics and Music*. London: Continuum, 2007.

Harnoncourt, Nikolaus. *Baroque Music Today: Music As Speech. Ways to a New Understanding of Music*. Translated by Mary O'Neill. Portland: Amadeus Press, 1982.

Heuguet, Guillaume (2016). "YouTube, la musique et moi." In *Où va la musique? Numérimorphose et nouvelles expériences d'écoute*, edited by Philippe Le Guern, 141–152. Paris: Presses des Mines, 2016.

Icard, Forence and Serfaty Marianne. "Études et recherche à la Hadopi: retour d'expérience sur l'observation des pratiques culturelles dématérialisées." In *En quête de musique. Questions de méthode à l'ère de la numérimorphose*, edited by Philippe Le Guern, 145–163. Paris: Hermann, 2017.

Ingarden, Roman. *The Literary Work of Art*. Translated by George G. Grabowicz. Evanston, Illinois: Northwestern University Press, 1973.

Ingarden, Roman. *The Work of Music and the Problem of Its Identity*. Translated from Polish by Adam Czerniawski. Edited by Jean G. Harrell. Houndmills: Macmillan, 1986.

Julien, Olivier. "'A Lucky Man Who Made the Grade:' Sgt. Pepper and the Rise of a Phonographic Tradition in Twentieth- century Popular Music." In *Sgt. Pepper and the Beatles, It Was forty Years Ago Today*, edited by Olivier Julien, 147–169. Aldershot: Ashgate, 2008.

Kania, Andrew. "Making Tracks: The Ontology of Rock Music." *The Journal of Aesthetics and Art Criticism* 64, n. 4 (2006): 401–414.

Kania, Andrew. "The Methodology of Musical Ontology: Descriptivism and its Implications." *British Journal of Aesthetics* 48, n. 4 (2008): 426–444.

Kania, Andrew. "New Waves in Musical Ontology." In *New Waves in Aesthetics*, edited by Kathleen Stock and Katherine Thomson-Jones. New York: Palgrave Macmillan, 2008.

Kania, Andrew. "Works, Recordings, Performances: Classical, Rock, Jazz." In *Recorded Music. Philosophical and Critical Reflections*, edited by Mine Dogantan-Dack, 3–21. London: Middlesex University Press, 2008.

Kania, Andrew. "All Play and No Works." *The Journal of Aesthetics and Art Criticism* 69, n. 4 (2011): 391–403.

Kania, Andrew, "The Philosophy of Music." *The Stanford Encyclopedia of Philosophy* (Fall 2012 Edition), edited by Edward N. Zalta. http://plato.stanford.edu/archives/fall2012/entries/music/.

Kania, Andrew. "Silent Music." *Journal of Aesthetics and Art Criticism* 68 n. 4 (2010): 343–353.

Kania, Andrew and Gracyk, Theodore. "Performances and Recordings." In *The Routledge Companion to Philosophy and Music*, edited by Andrew Kania and Theodore Gracyk, 80–90. London and New York: Routledge, 2011.

Kant, Immanuel. *Critique of Judgement*. Translated by James Creed Meredith. Revised, edited, and introduced by Nicholas Walker. Oxford and New York: Oxford University Press, 2007.

Katz, Mark. *Capturing Sound: How Technology Has Changed Music.* Berkeley and Los Angeles: University of California Press, 2010.

Killin, Anton. "Fictionalism about Musical Works." *Canadian Journal of Philosophy* 48 (2017): 266–91.

Kivy, Peter. "Platonism in Music: A Kind of Defense." *Grazer Philosophische Studien* 19 (1983): 109–29.

Kivy, Peter. *Authenticities: Philosophical Reflections on Musical Performance*. Ithaca: Cornell University Press, 1995.

Kivy, Peter. *Introduction to a Philosophy of Music*. Oxford: Clarendon Press, 2002.

Kobau, Pietro. "Parerga." *Rivista di Estetica*, 40 n. 1 (2009): 21–39.

Lai, Antonio. *Recherche et création entre tradition écrite et tradition orale: pour une nouvelle musique sarde*, Mémoire d'Habilitation à diriger les recherches. Paris: Université de Paris 8, 2011.

Larson, Steve. "Composition Versus Improvisation?" *Journal of Music Theory* 49, 2 (Fall 2005): 241–275.

Le Guern, Philippe. "Irreversible. Musique et technologies en régime numérique." *Réseaux* 172 (2012): 31–64.

Le Guern, Philippe. "Introduction," in *Où va la musique? Numérimorphose et nouvelles expériences d'écoute*, edited by Philippe Le Guern, 13–45. Paris: Presses des Mines, 2016.

Lehmann, Harry. *Die digitale Revolution der Musik. Eine Musikphilosophie*. Mainz: Schott Music, 2012.

Lephay, Pierre-Emmanuel. "La prise de son et le mixage, éléments de l'interprétation: les exemples de Herbert von Karajan et de Glenn Gould." In *Musique et enregistrement*, edited by Pierre-Henry Frangne and Hervé Lacombe, 113–122. Rennes: Presses Universitaires de Rennes, 2014.

Lephay, Pierre-Emmanuel. "De l''enregistrement-témoignage' à l''enregistrement-objet' et vice-versa." In *Quand l'enregistrement change la musique*, edited by Alessandro Arbo and Pierre-Emmanuel Lephay, 39–65. Paris: Hermann, 2017.

Léveillé Gauvin, Hubert. "Drawing listener attention in popular music: Testing five musical features arising from the theory of attention economy." *Musicae Scientiae* 22, n. 3 (2018): 291–304.

Levinson, Jerrold. *Music, Arts, and Metaphysics. Essays in Philosophical Aesthetics*. Oxford: Oxford University Press, 2011.

Levinson, Jerrold. *Musical Concerns. Essays in Philosophy of Music*. Oxford: Oxford University Press, 2015.

Levinson, Jerrold. "In Defense of Authenticity: Adjust Your Ears, Not the Music." In *Of Essence and Context. Between Music and Philosophy*, edited by Ruta Staneviciute, Nick Zangwill, & Rima Povilioniene, 185–195. New York: Springer, 2019.

London, Justin. "Ephemeral Media, Ephemeral Works, and Sonny Boy Williamson's 'Little Village'," *The Journal of Aesthetics and Art Criticism* 71 n. 1 (2013): 45–53.

Maestri, Eric. "Si può interpretare la musica elettroacustica?" In *Aisthesis* 6 (Special issue: *Ontologie musicali*, edited by Alessandro Arbo and Alessandro Bertinetto) (2013): 173–193. http://www.fupress.net/index.php/aisthesis/article/view/14101.

Magaudda, Paolo, *Oggetti da ascoltare. Hifi, iPod e consumo delle tecnologie musicali*, Bologna: il Mulino, 2012.

Marconi, Diego. "Artefatti e oggetti sociali." In *Ermeneutica, estetica, ontologia. A partire da Maurizio Ferraris*, edited by Tiziana Andina and Carola Barbero, 213–223. Bologna: il Mulino, 2016.

Matheson, Carl and Caplan, Ben. "Ontology." In *The Routledge Companion of Philosophy and Music*, edited by Theodore Gracyk and Andrew Kania, 38–47. London and New York: Routledge, 2011.

Michaud, Yves. *Critères esthétiques et jugement de goût*. Paris: Jacqueline Chambon, 1999.

Molino, Jean. "Technologie, mondialisation tribalisation. Un survol rétrospectif du XXe siècle." In *Musiques: une encyclopédie pour le XXIe siècle. 1. Musiques du XXe siècle*, edited by Jean-Jacques Nattiez, 69–86. Arles and Paris: Actes Sud and Cité de la musique, 2003.

Molino, Jean. "Qu'est-ce que l'oralité musicale?" In *Musiques. Une encyclopédie pour le 21e siècle. Vol. V L'unité de la musique,* edited by Jean-Jacques Nattiez, 477–527. Arles and Paris: Actes Sud and Cité de la musique, 2007.

Molino, Jean. *Le singe musicien. Essais de sémiologie et d'anthropologie de la musique*. Arles: Actes Sud, 2009.

Morizot, Jacques. "Œuvre." In *Dictionnaire d'esthétique et de philosophie de l'art*, edited by Jacques Morizot and Roger Pouivet, 337–338. Paris: Armand Colin, 2012[2].

Motta, Sébastien. "Rock Ontologie." *La vie des Idées* (2010) http://www.laviedesidees.fr/Rock-Ontologie.html.

Nattiez, Jean-Jacques. "Pluralité et diversité du savoir musical." In *Musiques. Une encyclopédie pour le XXIe siècle. 2 Les savoirs musicaux*, edited by Jean-Jacques Nattiez, 17–44. Arles/Paris: Actes Sud/Cité de la musique, 2004.

Nattiez, Jean-Jacques. "Interprétation et authenticité." In *Musiques. Une encyclopédie pour le XXIe siècle. 2 Les savoirs musicaux*, edited by Jean Jacques Nattiez, 1128–1148. Arles and Paris: Actes Sud and Cité de la Musique, 2004.

Ong, Walter. *Orality and Literacy: the Technologizing of the World*. London and New York: Methuen, 1982.

Orcalli, Angelo. "Recorded music: from the ethics of preservation to the critical editing." In *Sounds, Voices and Codes From the Twentieth Century. The Critical Editing of Music at Mirage*, edited by Luca Cossettini and Angelo Orcalli, 3–81. Udine: Mirage, 2017.

Pardo Salgado, Carmen. *Approche de John Cage. L'écoute oblique*. Translated (in French) by Nathalie Lhuillier and Hélène Olivesi. Paris: L'Harmattan, 2007.

Perticoz, Lucien. "Opulence musicale et recommandation. Quelques réserves fa e à une 'révolution' en cours." In *Où va la musique? Numérimorphose et nouvelles expériences d'écoute*, edited by Philippe Le Guern, 127–140. Paris: Presses des Mines, 2016.

Pestelli, Carlo. *Bella ciao: la canzone della libertà*. Torino: Add, 2016.

Piana, Giovanni. *Filosofia della musica*. Milano: Guerini, 1990.

Pouillaude, Frédéric. "D'une graphie qui ne dit rien. Les ambiguïtés de la notation chorégraphique." *Poétique* n° 137, n. 1 (2004): 99–123.

Pouivet, Roger. *L'œuvre d'art à l'âge de sa mondialisation, une ontologie de l'art de masse*. Bruxelles: La lettre volée, 2003.

Pouivet, Roger. *Qu'est-ce qu'une œuvre d'art?* Paris: Presses Universitaires de France, 2007.

Pouivet, Roger. *Philosophie du rock. Une ontologie des artefacts et des enregistrements*. Paris: Presses Universitaires de France, 2010.

Pouivet, Roger. "Les oeuvres musicales existent-elles? Un dialogue ontologique." In *Ontologie musicale: perspectives et débat*, edited by Alessandro Arbo and Marcello Ruta, 13–32. Paris: Hermann, 2014.

Pouivet, Roger. "La triple ontologie des deux sortes d'enregistrements musicaux." In *Musique et enregistrement*, edited by Pierre-Henry Frangne and Hervé Lacombe, 159–172. Rennes: Presses Universitaires de Rennes, 2014.

Predelli, Stefano, "Goodman and the Wrong Note Paradox." *British Journal of Aesthetics* 39 (1999): 364–75.

Pseudo-Plutarch. *Plutarch's Morals*. Translated by several hands, corrected and revised by William W. Goodwin. Boston: Little, Brown, and Company. Cambridge: Press of John Wilson and Son, 1874.

Quine, Willard Van Orman. *Ontological Relativity and Other Essays*. New York: Columbia University Press, 1969.

Ridley, Aaron. "Against Musical Ontology." *The Journal of Philosophy* 4 (2003): 203–230.

Riemann, Hugo. *Musikalishe Logik. Hauptzüge der physiologischen und psychologischen Begründung unseres Musiksystems*. Leipzig: Kahnt, 1874.

Rohrbaugh, Guy. "Artworks as Historical Individuals." *European Journal of Philosophy* 11 (2003): 177–205.

Rust, Joshua. *John Searle and The Construction of Social Reality*. London and New York: Continuum, 2006.

Ruta, Marcello. "Is there an Ontological Musical Common Sense?" *Aisthesis. Pratiche, linguaggi e saperi dell'estetico* (Special issue: *Ontologie musicali*, edited by Alessandro Arbo and Alessandro Bertinetto) 6 (2013): 67–86.

Schaeffer, Pierre. *Treatise on Musical Objects. An Essay across Disciplines*. Translated by Christine North and John Dack. Oakland: University of California Press, 2017.

Schaeffer, Jean-Marie. *Les célibataires de l'Art. Pour une esthétique sans mythes*. Paris: Gallimard, 1996.

Scherzinger, Martin. "Perceptual Modeling in the Era of Music's Automation." Unpublished. In *Conference of the "Società Italiana di Musicologia"*. Matera: Università della Basilicata, 19 octobre 2019.

Schütz, Alfred. "Making Music Together. A Study in Social Relationship." *Social Research* 18, n. 1–4 (1951): 76–97.

Schweikard, David P. and Hans Bernhard Schmid. "Collective Intentionality." *The Stanford Encyclopedia of Philosophy* (Winter 2020 Edition). Edited by Edward

N. Zalta. URL: https://plato.stanford.edu/archives/win2020/entries/collective-intentionality/.

Scruton, Roger. *The Aesthetics of Music*. Oxford: Clarendon, 1997.

Searle, John. *La construction de la réalité sociale*. New York: The Free Press, 1995.

Seashore, Carl E. *Psychology of Music*. New York: Dover, 1938.

Seidel, Wilhelm. *Werk und Werkbegriff in der Musikgeschichte*. Darmstadt: Wissenschaftliche Buchgesellschaft, 1987.

Sève, Bernard. *L'instrument de musique. Une étude philosophique*. Paris: Seuil, 2013.

Small, Christopher. *Musicking. The Meaning of Performing and Listening*. Middletown: Wesleyan University Press, 1998.

Solomos, Makis. *De la musique au son. L'émergence du son dans la musique des XXe–XXIe siècles*. Rennes: Presses Universitaires de Rennes, 2013.

Spade, Paul Vincent. "Do Composers Have To Be Performers Too?" *Journal of Aesthetics and Art Criticism* 49 (1991): 365–9.

Stecker, Robert. "Methodological Questions about the Ontology of Music." *Journal of Aesthetics and Art Criticism* 67 (2009): 375–386.

Sterne, Jonathan, *MP3: The Meaning of a Format. Sign, Storage, Transmission*. Durham: Duke University Press, 2012.

Stolnitz, Jerome. *Aesthetics and Philosophy of Art Criticism*. Boston: Houghton Mifflin, 1960.

Strawson, Peter Frederick. *Individuals: An Essay in Descriptive Metaphysics*. London and New York: Routledge, 1959.

Striphas, Ted. "Algorithmic culture." *European Journal of Cultural Studies* 18 (2015): 395–412.

Sulaiman Marion-Gallois, Saama. "Le rôle du disque dans la promotion et la pérennité d'un paradigme interprétatif." In *Quand l'enregistrement change la musique*, edited by Alessandro Arbo and Pierre-Emmanuel Lephay, 69–90. Paris: Hermann, 2017.

Thom, Paul. *For an Audience: A Philosophy of the Performing Arts*. Philadelphia: Temple University Press, 1993.

Thomasson, Amie L., "Ingarden and the Ontology of Cultural Objects." In *Existence, Culture, Persons: The Ontology of Roman Ingarden*, edited by Arkadiusz Chrudzimski, 115–136. Frankfurt: Ontos, 2005.

Tiffon, Vincent. "La partition, le phonographe et l'échantillonneur: usages de la copie en musique." *Déméter* (2003), 1–13. http://www.univ-lille3.fr/revues/demeter/copie/tiffon.pdf.

Tiffon, Vincent. "Pour une médiologie musicale comme mode original de connaissance." *Filigrane* 1 (2005): 115–139.

Tournès, Ludovic. *Musique! Du phonographe au MP3*. Paris: Editions Autrement, 2011.

Valéry, Paul. "La conquête de l'ubiquité (1928)." In *Œuvres. Tome II: Pièces sur l'art*. Paris: Gallimard 1960: 1283–1287.

Vernallis, Carol. *Unruly Media: YouTube, Music Video, and the New Digital Cinema*. New York: Oxford University Press, 2013.

Volcler, Juliette. *Contrôle. Comment s'inventa l'art de la manipulation sonore*. Paris: Cité de la musique/Philarmonie de Paris, 2017.

Walton, Kendall Lewis. "Categories of Art." *The Philosophical Review* 79/3 (1970), 334–367.

Weil, Rodolphe. "Entre œuvre phonographique et improvisation: le cas du dub." In *Quand l'enregistrement change la musique*, edited by Alessandro Arbo and Pierre-Emmanuel Lephay, 153–170. Paris: Hermann, 2017.

Weiss Hanrahan, Nancy. "La découverte musicale en régime numérique." In: *Où va la musique? Numérimorphose et nouvelles expériences d'écoute*, edited by Philippe Le Guern, 65–80. Paris: Presses des Mines, 2016.

Wiora, Walter. *Das musikalische Kunstwerk*. Tutzing: Hans Schneider, 1983.

Wittgenstein, Ludwig. *Lectures and Conversations on Aesthetics, Psychology and Religious Belief*. Edited by Cyril Barrett. Berkeley and Los Angeles: University of California Press, 1967.

Wolff, Francis. *Pourquoi la musique*. Paris: Fayard, 2015.

Wollheim, Richard. *Art and Its Objects. Second edition*. Cambridge: Cambridge University Press, 1980.

Wolterstorff, Nicholas. *Works and Worlds of Art*. Oxford: Clarendon, 1980.

Young, James O. "The Poverty of Music Ontology." *Journal of Music and Meaning* 13 (2014), 1–19.

www.ingramcontent.com/pod-product-compliance
Lightning Source LLC
Chambersburg PA
CBHW031327230926
51848CB00001B/125